WE
ALL
GO
INTO
THE
DARK

FRANCISCO GARCIA

WE ALL GO INTO THE DARK

The Hunt for
Bible John

MUDLARK

Mudlark
HarperCollins*Publishers*
1 London Bridge Street
London SE1 9GF
www.harpercollins.co.uk

HarperCollins*Publishers*
Macken House, 39/40 Mayor Street Upper
Dublin 1, D01 C9W8, Ireland

First published by Mudlark 2023
1 3 5 7 9 10 8 6 4 2

Text © Francisco Garcia 2023

Photographs on pages 45, 79, 107 and 120: Mirrorpix; page 62:
PA Images/Alamy Stock Photo

Francisco Garcia asserts the moral right to be
identified as the author of this work

A catalogue record of this book is available from the British Library

ISBN 978-0-00-853145-4

Printed and bound in the UK using 100% renewable electricity
at CPI Group (UK) Ltd

This book is produced from independently certified FSC™ paper to
ensure responsible forest management.

For more information visit: www.harpercollins.co.uk/green

To my family

At last the lamps go too, when fog
drives monstrous down the dual carriageway
out to the west, and even in my room
and on this paper I do not know
about that grey dead pane
of ice that sees nothing and that nothing sees.

EDWIN MORGAN, 'Winter (EM)'

CONTENTS

WE ALL GO INTO THE DARK

PROLOGUE

There was a moment in the mid-1970s, a fragile, vanishing moment, when it must have seemed like the future was coming to Stonehouse.

The sleepy South Lanarkshire village sits around half an hour's drive south-east of Glasgow on the banks of the Avon Water, the picturesque river that snakes its way across Scotland's inner west coast before eventually running into the River Clyde by a nameless stretch of land just off the M74 motorway. Though surrounded by rolling green hills, the main body of the village itself occasionally carries a heavy-set feeling of isolation depending on the season. There are times under the winter rain, for instance, when the rows of thin grey buildings appear to be bleeding, as if slashed by an unseen knife.

Stonehouse has had its own modest claims to renown over a long and occasionally difficult history. From the

1

mid-eighteenth century, it was synonymous with the output of its weavers and, in particular, for their work with silk, including the fine scarves and handkerchiefs produced for export to India. A century later, it was often said by local observers that the patterns spun by a Stonehouse master were more delicate than anything that had ever been conceived of before in Scotland. These boom years saw the village expand, with entire new streets of handsome, privately built cottages arriving to support its growing population. Many of these buildings endure. Hill Road, Camnethan Street and Queen Street exist almost unchanged to this day, as part of the village's proudly maintained and manicured conservation area.

The decline, when it unfolded, was gradual rather than precipitous. Despite the damage wrought by advancing technology there were plenty of handloom weavers who still persisted in the old ways. They adapted, or tried to adapt, as best they could, until even the guarantee of their craftsmanship was no protection against the heavy, inexorable march of progress. By the end of the nineteenth century, coal mining had begun to dominate, until it too bedded down into a joyless terminal decline. The last colliery in the area was shut in 1958, though its legacy is felt to this day in the twisted bones of the subsiding properties in its vicinity. The close of the decade marked the shift into a new world, riven with uncertainty. It wasn't tough to catch the melancholic symbolism a year later, with the death of the last weaver in Lanarkshire, 84-year-old James Hamilton of Camnethan Street, Stonehouse.

The following years saw a sense of isolation set in. For some, this was a source of comfort. The retreat into a blanket of well-worn custom, where change remained a process to be measured in reassuringly gradual increments, running into one another unseen over the blurred weeks and months, the long years and decades. But Stonehouse never quite became a tomb. It wasn't unheard of for people to still move to the village and make their lives there, though few ever made the mistake of considering themselves anything other than benignly tolerated outsiders. To truly be from Stonehouse remained a question of generational roots, of being able to trace the thread back, right back, into the dimly lit or otherwise forgotten past. One might live, work and drink there for decades. But without that thread, one might only ever achieve a foreigner's status.

This was due to change on 10 May 1976, the day that the future was officially unveiled in Stonehouse. Thirty years earlier had seen the publication of the Clyde Valley Regional Plan, a visionary argument in favour of easing Glasgow's perilous housing crisis by decamping a quarter of its million inhabitants into freshly constructed 'New Towns'. Stonehouse was designated as the sixth of its kind, with 22,000 new homes under construction for the 35,000 Glaswegian incomers earmarked for arrival. There would be jobs, thousands of stable, well-paid, usually vaguely defined jobs, to go around, located at the four new 'employment parks'. There would be investment. New schools, leisure centres and a freshly reopened train line to connect Stonehouse to the rest of the West Coast and beyond.

Photos survive of the bright May morning when the first families moved into the neat rows of modernist semi-detached houses on Murray Drive, a freshly constructed cul-de-sac replete with its own carefully built-in islands of green space. One can still see the beaming children in tartan flares and Sunday-best woollen jumpers, walking hand-in-hand with pin-striped local dignitaries. Severe, slightly dazed-looking mothers with wind-swept bobs jostle at the edges of the frame, looking as if they can't quite believe in the reality of the day unfolding before them. There were speeches and a lengthy ceremony to mark the arrival of the city families and this fresh, brilliant chapter in the village's history.

Two days later and hundreds of miles south in London, the then Secretary of State for Scotland, Bruce Millan, stood up in the House of Commons to announce that the further development of Stonehouse was to be immediately abandoned, despite the already existing £4,000,000 outlay. The ex-mining village in South Lanarkshire was no longer needed now that Glasgow's population had begun to shrink sharply of its own accord, after a painful decade of decline. And just like that, the future drifted somewhere else. Not everyone was disheartened by the news. Opposition to the New Town plans had been vocal and well organized. Local farmers had been forced to cede significant chunks of land, while some inhabitants fretted about the social impact of tens of thousands of incomers from the dark, dangerous city to the north. Things carried on, much as they always had. Life in Stonehouse continued to run to its own specific rhythm, at its slightly removed distance from much of the rest of the surrounding world. Half a century on, some have still not quite been able to let go of the sequence of missed opportunities. Today, the once unfathomably modern local authority houses on Murray Drive still exist almost unchanged from their construction, if a little worn from the wear and tear of the passing decades. But the New Town debacle wasn't the last time Stonehouse made the national press in the latter half of the twentieth century.

The first day of February 1996. Everyone agrees about the cold that morning. The ugly, numbing cold that cut across the fields surrounding Stonehouse Cemetery, a few hundred yards from the heart of the village. The real work began at 9.07 a.m., when the first pneumatic drills began to scrape and bite at the frozen grave sheltered under a hastily erected white marquee. Despite the whine of the blades chipping against the soil, there was still a feeling of uneasy repose blended into the faint hum of motorway traffic to the north. Uniformed police stood by listening to the machinery at work on the other side of the thin layer of white plastic, while council workmen in navy boiler suits and medical masks filtered in and out of the tent. The exhumation had begun.

A green Peugeot idled along the single track by the cemetery gates before pulling up to park. Three plain-clothes officers made their way to the workmen, before stopping to talk with a blonde woman in her mid-thirties, clad in a thick, brown, fur-trimmed coat with a small rectangular case at her feet. Dr Marie Cassidy had been there since dawn, supervising preparations. The forensic pathologist was accompanied by Professor Anthony Busuttil, one of the most senior medical figures in the country. The white tent was carefully spread across half a dozen graves, an area marked by a precise measure of light-coloured tape. Though broadly to protect the surrounding plots, the construction had another purpose. The press had begun to arrive not long after first light, with a steady stream of reporters and news crews angling against the cold, jostling desperately for the best shot of the unfolding action, or a few clipped, cagey quotes from the more senior police officers present. Before the tent's entrance was hurriedly fastened and the drills began to tear down through the frost-covered soil, the hungry expectant eyes of the assembled journalists were drawn to a single unassuming headstone, covering a family plot occupied by a father, mother and son. After the drills came the shovels, the council workmen sweating under portable gas heaters as the earth finally began to yield. Two hours later, the mother's coffin was removed and transported to a local funeral parlour. Another hour passed before the real prize was uncovered. The second coffin – the son's – was delicately shrouded with white cloth and placed in the back of a silver Volvo saloon, to be transported to Glasgow City Mortuary where the rounds of forensic testing were to begin immediately.

By evening, the exhumation was all over the TV news. The BBC anchor put it simply enough, in reassuringly bland professional tones, flanked by a black-and-white photofit of a strange, ageless figure with a jutting chin and lifeless, lightless eyes.

Police have exhumed the body of a man they believe was the notorious serial killer Bible John. Detectives in Strathclyde want to prove that John McInnes, who committed suicide 16 years ago, was the man who murdered three Glasgow women in the late

1960s. Recent DNA tests have linked him to one of the victims.

Over on ITV, *Scotland Today* led the programme with the day's revelations.

First tonight, pathologists are beginning tests on the man police believe may be Bible John. The remains of John McInnes were dug up from the grave he shared with his parents at Stonehouse Cemetery late this morning.

Tight security surrounded the five-hour operation which began at dawn. Police now hope scientific tests will bring to an end a 27-year murder mystery.

* * *

Always the same answer, time and again, without fail. Yes, I'm writing about Bible John, I explain to anyone polite enough to have asked me about the book I've been working on these past couple of years. The reaction mostly depends on who I'm talking with and where we are. At home in London, it usually tends to alternate between tolerant incomprehension or the odd pleasantly vague nod of recognition, as if at the reminder of a long-forgotten guilty midnight Wikipedia spree. Then come the quickly disguised looks of pity and alarm (and yes, sometimes fascination too), before my interlocutor fights their way back to the bar for a suddenly urgent round. Another man writing another serial-killer story. A story that sees three women murdered and discarded in back closes and dingy alleys, their killer never caught or brought to anything approaching justice. I have learned to clam up, to keep quiet or bluster around the subject until conversation can be safely moved on to something with less self-evident potential for crankishness.

This isn't always the case in Glasgow, though certainly there is some of the same slightly repelled push-and-pull. Bible John means something different here. This is, after all, where the killings took place, spread over the twenty-one months between February 1968 and November 1969. They were certainly not the only murders to have taken place there in that period. Indeed, most histories point to a particularly troubled time in a particularly volatile city, with a murder rate twice that of London's during the same decade (this has passed into gospel, despite the problems in accurate statistical comparison).

If violence was a casual, unremarkable part of the texture of life in some areas of 1960s Glasgow, what arrived with Bible John appeared to be something new. Murder had long been understood to follow a certain set of imprecisely defined rules. It was a matter for the young and untameable, or the city's more organized criminal fraternity. The usual killings, both random and planned. People killed at parties that had turned sour over a stray remark, or young men stabbed to death during street warfare. The murders that no one could muster up too much surprise at. Crimes that cropped up with increasing frequency. Elderly spinsters discovered with their heads caved in in their own homes, or young women dumped in the grounds of suburban cemeteries. To some, they seemed to reflect something inherent to the times; something about the growing alarm of life lived in a city self-consciously lurching into modernity. For others, the killings spoke for themselves and needed no further explanation.

There had been other infamous killings in the city's recent, or recentish, history. Peter Manuel was a housebreaker and petty thief, who had served nine years in Peterhead Prison for violent sexual assault as a young man, before becoming the kind of killer that no one had really seen before. He killed seven people in 1958 and likely more. The murders were random and didn't seem to follow anything like a set pattern. He bludgeoned his victims and strangled them. He shot families in their homes and stalked women across suburban golf courses.

At his trial, the judge opined that he was very bad without being mad. There was a lot to be written and said about Peter Manuel, though nothing that has ever served as a key to unlocking some secret explanation for the terrible, pointless violence. The sheer weight and randomness of it. The trial in Glasgow was a media and cultural sensation. It ran and ran in the papers of the day and ended with the killer being hanged, the last criminal to ever be legally executed in Glasgow and the third last in Scotland as a whole.

The Barrowland Ballroom murders were to be different. Between February 1968 and the early hours of November 1969, three women were killed after a night spent at the famous dancehall in the city's East End. The first two killings were separated by almost eighteen months, while less than three months separated the final two. The women had several things in common, and many other things apart. They were all mothers over the age of 25. They were all entirely unknown to one another. They each had dark hair and were found to be menstruating at the time of their death. Their bodies were discovered near their respective homes, in the south, east and west of the city. They were each badly beaten and then strangled. The majority of accounts also insist that they were raped, though no convincing proof has ever been found to corroborate this.

By the end of 1969, it was thought to be increasingly certain that all three had been killed by the same man – red-haired, sharp-suited, scripture-quoting – though he was already in the process of becoming something slightly more than a man by then. This was the figure that the press had christened 'Bible John', a moniker dreamed up from the few thin scraps of information provided by the only surviving eyewitness to spend significant time with the apparent serial killer. No one then could have suspected the enduring impact of these three specific crimes. At the start, there was nothing to suggest these were to be anything other than a further addition to the constantly growing pile of murder files spread across the desks of detectives around the city.

But as the weeks became months, and the months became years, the three killings were to remain unsolved. The files remain open today over half a century on, though the women's – the *victims'* – lives have mostly receded from view, dominated by the weight of speculation that came to lie on their deaths. Bible John was to become a folk devil; a particularly vicious spooky story to shock recalcitrant children or serve as the perfect conversational fodder to fill sad, half-cut hours in pubs around the city. But that was later. At the start, there was a different intensity. For a time at the very beginning of the 1970s, it felt to many as if much of the city couldn't

really breathe with the killer uncaught. Suspicion hung in
the air. It squatted in bus shelters and shadowed door-
ways. In short, it flourished, like snowdrops under the
first spring sun.

And when the murders appeared to have stopped, the
fear they occasioned didn't. With the man, the figure,
uncaught there was always the possibility he could kill
again. Horror is often easily explicable. A man who con-
fesses to strangling his wife in a jealous rage, or the
teenager discovered with a bloody knife after killing
another boy over a territorial dispute centred on a few
streets of this or that housing scheme on the outer fringes
of the city. Predictable faces matched to predictable
crimes. Stuck on the same endlessly disappointing loop.
But Bible John, the uncaught killer, would offer something different and his power has never quite been
banished or destroyed.

Many people have written about Bible John, some well
and others badly. There have been TV documentaries and
impassioned book-length studies published by the tiniest
vanity presses. The mystery is like a clarion call to all
sorts of people, with all sorts of motives. I like to think
I've read and watched them all, or at least the vast majority. They range from the fairly sober and factual to the
wild and, occasionally, potently deranged. They contain
the same revolving cast of ex-police figures and mildly

notorious talking heads. They offer theories and conjecture. They name names. The new suspects who have flitted in and out of vogue. Like John McInnes, the ex-squaddie exhumed from Stonehouse Cemetery in 1996. Like Peter Tobin, the 60-year-old serial killer captured in the mid-2000s for a totally unrelated series of crimes. Like Fred West, or Peter Sutcliffe, or any other notorious murderer who might, or might not, have been in Glasgow at the time of the killings. A revolving cast of human depravity, offered up for casual inspection. It can seem as if everyone with an interest in the story has an opinion, which freely jump from the plausible to the abjectly fantastical.

There are those who owe their career, or part of it, to such speculation. Celebrity criminologists who have hoovered up press coverage through their accusations, or long-retired former detectives from the era who have memoirs to promote. It takes a different form for others. A hobby unsullied by any idea of material reward. The amateur sleuths who diligently tend to the Reddit pages and lovingly crafted blogs devoted to Bible John and the theories regarding his identity.

It's rarely simple trying to dissect the reasons behind settling down to write a book, particularly one on a quasi-mythical serial killer 'active' over half a century ago, in a city at the other end of the UK from the one I call home.

Fascination, disgust, a certain strain of morbid curiosity. These have all factored into it. As has a nagging feeling somewhere at the back of my mind since I started reporting on the story in the summer of 2018, on a week-long trip I'd made to Glasgow to cover the fiftieth anniversary of the killings. That, among the apparently endless reams of newsprint and stilted documentary footage, there might still be something interesting and fresh to say about Bible John. I confess that I can't remember when I first heard about the story, but it must have happened during the year I spent in Glasgow as a master's student living in Dennistoun out in the East End, not too far from The Barrowland Ballroom, the venue that all three of the victims had spent their final nights at before slipping into Glaswegian mythology along with their killer. I'd like to write that there was a specific moment when my interest ignited, some kind of easily dramatizable flash of recognition or neatly poetic event that set me onto a story that I've not ever really been able to entirely shake since. Though that wouldn't be true. I don't make this as an admission of any special individual moral clarity. Only as a reminder to myself that Bible John certainly isn't a tale that needs any more wilful falsehoods or strategic embellishment inserted into it.

One reason for my sustained interest resides in the paucity of the coverage of the three women's lives. The three women killed. Patricia Docker, Jemima MacDonald and Helen Puttock. We will get to this – to them – in much greater detail soon enough. In the years of my research and reporting, this problem hasn't simply resolved itself and there were moments when I became squeamish at the idea of contacting their surviving family members, so long after they had their wives and mothers, sisters and aunts so violently taken from them. It's not a moral question I think can be answered to anyone's great satisfaction, least of all my own. There is also the question of what Bible John has come to represent, to different people, across different decades in a rapidly changing Glasgow. To the Glaswegians of the late 1960s, this very modern kind of killer came to seem like a judgement. A verdict on what was increasingly thought of by some to be a loose and depraved working-class immorality, reflecting a city in flux, shifting into a strange and some-times frightening future. And this, too, we will arrive at later, through a mist of obfuscation. Through a fatally flawed initial police investigation that sometimes owed more to the occult than it did to even the deeply imper-fect and flawed procedure of its era. And how those same flaws have barely been addressed in the decades since.

It was the press that created Bible John and the press that have kept the name alive. One has (as I have) to recognize the irony in this, writing this at my desk piled in old papers and barely decipherable notes, by adding another offering to the vast and swollen Bible John bibliography. I offer no pretence that my contribution will help finally solve the mystery at the heart of the story. For many, the best informed and most obsessive included, that is not an ending within anyone's reach. Instead, I have combed through archives and interviewed many of the people still living who have a connection to the killings and their reverberations, as well as those who hold what I've taken to be a unique or just an outsized fascination in this collision of myth and very real, very tangible violence. I have not ignored the chasm that separates me from the crimes or the era they were committed in. Equally, I have tried to avoid pointless self-flagellation. Instead, I have done my best to remain confident that the same gap might have allowed me to facilitate new angles of approach and suggest fresh ways of attacking the crumpled old case files.

The result is what I hope is an honest attempt to swim in the cold, damp spaces between verifiable fact and convenient fiction. To reanimate something of what Bible John meant to the lives of those who were there to bear witness to the initial hysteria and its subsequent passing into legend. To bring some forgotten truths back into focus and tear apart the more useless, or harmful, lies that have surrounded it. And not least, to try and understand why some killings are forgotten with occasionally indecent haste and others are never quite permitted to be forgotten at all.

THE DANCING

The Barrowland Ballroom sits at 244 Gallowgate, out on the inner-city fringes of Glasgow's East End. Arriving from the city centre today will take you past a blur of tenement blocks and phone repair shops, thinly stocked Polish supermarkets and the occasional pub draped in the loudest imaginable Celtic FC iconography. Even on the most soporific midweek afternoon, the venue is impossible to miss. To its right stands a new and self-consciously trendy bar painted a soberly matted black, which is physically connected to the wrought-iron archway entrance to the next-door Barras market. To its immediate left lurks a thin and unprepossessing side street harbouring another bar and a couple of small, slightly ambiguous businesses.

The best way to approach the Barrowland is by foot. That way there is the pleasingly sudden shift in perspective from a landscape of low-rise individual units into something altogether larger, brasher and unapologetically self-confident. It isn't that the Barrowland glitters during daylight hours. Instead, six metallic-grey shuttered doors run across the ground floor, the facade of which alternates between short bursts of marble by the main entrance and the more utilitarian pebble-dash which covers the rest. But these prissy details aren't what's likely to grab the attention of the first-time visitor. The Barrowland sign is an undeniably striking creation, with its fifteen-or-so feet of greyish green, smooth plastic panels which rise out from the entrance and spread twice as far wide. Lightbulb-covered metal stars in blue and white circle the bold lettering, with each individual letter studded with its own network of smaller individual bulbs. It's tough not to be impressed by the stark physical reality of a building that so thoroughly and carelessly dominates its immediate surroundings. From the cheerful red-and-white 1970s typography on a small incidental notice above the main door to the looming Americana-tinged presence of the main sign itself, there's a sometimes charming and often heavy feeling of a place existing out of time, even if it's hard to say precisely from outside which epoch it appears to be marooned in.

Somehow, these feelings are both more and less acute by night, when the electricity floods into the front of the building, illuminating the sign a stark shade of orange and bathing the pavement below in its sickly refracted light. The Barrowland is one of Scotland's most revered and storied music venues, shrouded with lore and finely honed anecdote, the weight of which might appear legendary or wearisome depending on an individual's capacity and tolerance for self-mythology.

From the mid-1970s onwards, it has hosted many of the world's best-known acts, an eclectic mismatch ranging from The Clash and David Bowie to The Smiths, Oasis, Britney Spears and U2. The venue's reputation is one of highly cultivated intensity. At a push, 1,900 people can be packed into the cavernous main hall, with its polished wood floors leading up to the main stage. At its highest pitch, the atmosphere has been known occasionally to curdle. In the late 1970s, the self-avowedly confrontational New York synthpunk double act Suicide began their set by goading the packed, already tense crowd. Not long into the set, frontman Alan Vega later reported watching an axe fly past his head. It was, he said, one of his favourite gigs in an almost half-century-long career. In 2013, a history of the venue's recent history was published. *Barrowland: A Glasgow Experience* by Nuala Naughton is a good-natured, if slightly self-congratulatory offering, featuring reminiscences from several of the bands who have played there repeatedly over the decades. Not every anecdote offers a paean to the Barrowland's fabled atmosphere or is simply content to 'wax lyrical about the sprung floor; the low ceiling; the sweat running down the walls; the ghosts of gigs past [or] the chintzy dressing room with its mirrors framed with a multitude of bare lightbulbs'.

There was a not-so-distant time when the security guards had a reputation for what could euphemistically be called heavy-handedness ('violence' works equally well here). JJ Burnel, bassist for The Stranglers, remembers confronting a bouncer who he'd seen laying into an audience member, while a roadie for American heavy metal act Anthrax recalls another doorman getting rough with a young female fan, until the band themselves stepped in. In the early 1990s, Zack de la Rocha of Rage Against the Machine jumped off stage to fly kick a bouncer who had set on another young fan. The chapter ends with Big Wullie Campbell, a self-described 'eviction technician' who admits with a wink and shrug that the bouncers were 'bullies', though times had changed by the early 2010s, even though 'he wouldn't say we turned into saints overnight'.

The idea for a venue on the site was first conceived in the early 1930s by 'The Barras Queen' Maggie McIver, the notoriously ruthless self-made East End entrepreneur, who had grown up hard scrap poor in the fading embers of Victorian Glasgow. Along with her husband, James, she was responsible for the birth of the Barras market just off the Gallowgate, which opened in the mid-1920s. Its major innovation came from being permanently covered, which guaranteed year-round trading, making the already wealthy family considerably richer.

Acquiring the previously unremarkable scrub of inner-city land hadn't been straightforward. The title had belonged to a wealthy elderly woman from what was then a particularly plush corner of the city's West End. Marion Gilchrist had lived alone at 5 Queen's Terrace on West Princes Street. On the night of 21 December 1908, she had sent a servant out for the evening paper. When the girl returned, she opened the door to witness a shadowy male figure flitting out of a bedroom and onto the street. Gilchrist was discovered face down in the drawing room with her skull caved in, lying inert in a pool of her own blood. The police were called, and the servant interrogated. A recently arrived German-Jewish immigrant named Oscar Slater was duly arrested and put on trial at the High Court in Edinburgh. After narrowly avoiding a death sentence, he was 'reprieved' and sentenced to penal servitude for life in 1909. To many contemporary observers, the 'Scottish Dreyfus case' had been a travesty and it refused to drift entirely from the public imagination. After a long and often bitterly intense public campaign, Slater eventually had his sentence quashed in 1928, after nineteen years in prison. He lived out the rest of his days in Ayrshire, having married a Scottish woman and opened an antiques business with his official compensation. He died in 1948 aged 79. Marion Gilchrist's murder remains unsolved, though a consensus has emerged over the decades that sudden changes to her will formed the likely motive.

The legal wrangles over her estate still hadn't been settled by the time the McIvers made their move on the murdered woman's land. But 'legal men's dilly-dallies were not Maggie's way', as one of her more excitable biographers puts it. As the newly built market began to thrive, she turned to her next venture. Having gained experience renting out public halls to run 'dinner dances' for her loyal stallholders, McIver began to calculate whether her Gallowgate property would support a hall of her own. After demolishing a row of dilapidated tenements, the original Barrowland Ballroom opened for its first dance on Christmas Eve 1934, built on the ashes of the former 'evil slums'. That first night had seen the drummer of the booked band taken ill. His replacement, Billy McGregor, would go on to lead the newly formed house band, The Gaybirds, with its sixteen-piece orchestra, their sets ranging from slow-burning waltzes to tangos, quicksteps and foxtrots. The venue was an instant success, at least on a par with the market next door. In the first half of the twentieth century, most working-class adults in Scotland divided their leisure time between the cinema and the dancing. Edinburgh's Assembly Rooms had been the first venue to hold public dances from the 1870s, while Glasgow's Albert Hall had the distinction of being the first purpose-built dancehall in the country when it opened in 1905.

By the 1930s, almost every city and town had its own dedicated venue. The names ranged from the functional and unimaginative (the Marine Ballroom in Arbroath, the severe north-east-coast fishing town) to the mildly zany (Oddfellows Hall in North Berwick, better known as The Sweatbox because of the fitted blackout curtains that trapped the Saturday night heat and sweat). In the remotest villages and inner cities alike, thousands of young people poured into the dancehalls for the chance to fleetingly forget the drudgery of work and domestic routine. Countless couples could trace their origins to a turn taken under the lights in their local dancehall. Silent, granular black-and-white footage survives of this often-invoked alleged 'golden age', the frame full of careless smiling figures moving to the enthusiastic strains of the resident big band. The men are invariably in their smartest suits, with the women in their finest dresses. The casual observer of these scenes would be forgiven for taking them to be the epitome of a lost and quasi-mythical wholesomeness.

Drink wasn't always a factor in these nights, though neither was it absent entirely. It depended on where you were. Or who. In *Are Ye Dancin'? The Story of Scotland's Dance Halls*, a woman named Shona Wallace remembers her youth in the West Highland town of Fort William. As a 19-year-old it was still a big deal, she explains, to leave her hometown, even just to cover the 10 or so miles to Ballachulish for a night at the dancing. There would always be someone from home there to observe her, ostensibly to make sure that none of the men she danced with had any more sinister designs. These nights were generally sober affairs. Wallace is firm in her recollections. Girls 'just didn't drink' in those days and those who did risked immediate censure. 'People would say the most awful things about you – especially if you were found drunk.'

Glasgow was increasingly saturated with venues, though perhaps this is hardly surprising considering its status as Scotland's largest city. But The Barrowland Ballroom had rapidly begun to acquire its own specific mystique. A programme for the Christmas 1935 season laid out its charms in rapturous prose.

To view the outside of Barrowland Palais de Danse at night makes one impatient for the enjoyments within ... Imagine a hall aglow with cunningly

concealed lights and a floor capable of holding a
thousand dancers ... the orchestra in scarlet uni-
forms of evening suit design, rendering their music
which is at once a pleasure and delight.

When war broke out in September 1939, legislation was
passed that ordered the shuttering of all public dancehalls, though it was rapidly overturned after a public
outcry (however, the Barrowland was asked to remove its
already famous neon sign). By then, word of the venue's
notoriety had apparently spread as far as Germany, where
'Lord Haw-Haw' made repeated reference to it in his
anti-British propaganda broadcasts. 'I know how well the
Barrowland people treat the French and American sol-
diers, and I hope they will do the same for the German
victors when they arrive in Scotland.' It's true that the
venue was particularly popular with American service-
men, and multiple sources credit the GIs with introducing
several strange and inexplicable new dance moves into
general circulation, including the jive and the jitterbug.
Surviving Pathé footage shows processions of ecstatic
young dancers, peeling off from one another on the
dancefloor in varying states of mania. 'It may surprise
you to know that this dance is done in Great Britain,'
intones the plummy unseen English narrator, 'but we are
the pictorial news and we are the news that includes

anything which is unusual.' By the end of the war, the Barrowland had its own cordoned-off section for the 'jitterbuggers', so as not to disturb the more traditional ballroom crowd. In one 1990s history of the Barrowland, a nameless 'Glasgow man' tells the story of his conception in 1944. Following his birth, he had been abandoned by his mother, though he was steadfast in believing his love of western films was an inherited characteristic, due to his American parentage. His mother, a Glaswegian, had been a regular at The Barrowland Ballroom during the war. He explains to the book's authors how he was certain that his father had been an American ranch-hand named Hank, who had a six-month relationship with his mother while stationed in Glasgow. He had discovered this by tracing his family through his maternal aunt, though his mother had died years before. The broader outline of this story was hardly unusual, whatever the truth of the man's own individual circumstances.

The Forties and Fifties passed by with the same ease and affluence. The McIver fortune increased, as weekend after weekend brought revellers from the city and beyond, with queues often snaking down the Gallowgate. Things changed with the fire. It was around 6 a.m. on 19 August 1958 when a nightwatchman discovered the first flames licking at the innards of the venue. It was, reporters from the city's tabloids wrote, 'one of the most spectacular blazes' seen in Glasgow in several decades. Families in the surrounding tenements were evacuated into the grey early morning drizzle, while over a hundred firefighters poured in from around the city. One woman reported being shaken out of her night's sleep by a watchman beating at the front door. 'When I heard the knock I thought at first there had been either a burst pipe or a gassing. I wakened my daughter and then I saw the fire. [She] had seen it earlier but thought she was dreaming.'

The *Glasgow Herald*, one of the city's more staid broadsheets, reported that fourteen detachments of the city's fire brigade were needed to quell the flames over two hours. Thousands of gallons of water were poured through onto the fire as it ate away at the building's structure, causing the roof to collapse forty-five minutes after the fire service's arrival. Onlookers reported a sound akin to a storm breaking. Over forty cars in the show-room below the main dancehall had to be pushed down the Gallowgate to East Campbell Street, while the morning's *Evening Times* ran with a photograph of the remains of a twisted saxophone that had been deformed by the fire. When the flames were finally quelled, little remained of the hall's original structure. There are images of sober, dark-suited firemen picking through the maimed limbs of the building and the surrounding wreckage, grasping at the ground for anything salvageable. Grotesquely distorted metal laps at the men's legs, as if possessed by a nameless hunger. The damage was calculated at £100,000, though the fire's origins were to remain a mystery (perhaps the most likely explanation has it originating in the tearoom). Maggie McIver's son, Sam (the old woman had died a few months before her life's work had gone up in flames), was quick to declare the family's intention to rebuild the dancehall. It wasn't – he proclaimed – a mere ballroom, like its innumerable competitors, but an institution.

The grand reopening took place on Christmas Eve 1960. Adverts ran for a Carnival Dance for Christmas Day and a Boxing Day dance. Admission was five shillings, and the music was provided by Billy McGregor & His Gaybirds, still at the peak of their celebrity. Temporary catastrophe aside, there was no reason yet to believe the fire to be anything other than a short-lived, if regrettable, interruption to a quarter-century's worth of previously unbroken prosperity. The new ceiling had been finished in dazzling 'midnight blue' and incorporated the stars which had dotted the old roof. Rumours circulated that the new dancefloor had been built with imported Canadian maple wood and layered underneath with thousands of halved tennis balls, placed to cushion the feet of dancers. Though the triumphant McIvers weren't to know it, the turn of the new decade represented the

peak for Glasgow's dancehalls. This was the age of The
Majestic Ballroom, The Cameo, The Locarno, The Tudor,
and The Astoria. Of F & F in Partick and Green's Play-
house at 126 Renfield Street in the city centre, which
hosted Joe Loss's internationally renowned big band for
a run every year. There was Warren's on Bath Street and
The Dennistoun Palais. The Tower Ballroom in Maryhill
and The Plaza down in the red sandstone suburbia of
Shawlands, in the Southside. Though each of these carried its own private and hard-fought-for slice of the
market, few could compare to the Barrowland in scale or
renown.

For one Glasgow musician, Bill Gracie, the beginning
of the end for the big band era could be traced to 1961,
the year after a pre-superstardom Beatles had embarked
on a tour of provincial theatres around Scotland. The
scene was changing. Though the ballrooms had weath-
ered the impact of the 1950s and its seismic changes to
youth culture, the emerging 'beat boom' offered another
challenge entirely. Gracie is quoted in *Are Ye Dancin'?* on
how he was told by the management of a Hamilton
dancehall that his band would have to share a set with a
local pop act. 'Things were happening quite slowly but I
think for the public the big changes were you didn't have
to buy a book full of dance steps, you didn't have to wear
your Sunday best and you could just jump about like a

demented dervish to pull the birds.' There were, he is quick to add, no long-lasting ill feelings.

It wasn't long before the closures began. First came the smaller or more remote venues. Slowly, even the Barrowland began to lose some of its sheen and long-cultivated glamour. As the weekly takings declined, another mood set in as its aura of respectability began to drain away. By the mid-1960s, there were increasingly loud mutterings about what the Barrowland was thought to be beginning to represent: a place to where married men and women, leaving their spouses at home for the night, would risk slipping down to the Gallowgate armed with an assumed name. Thursday nights took on a particular notoriety. These were the Over-25s nights, where wedding rings were casually slipped off before joining the queue. Violence was increasingly common. The city's tabloids excitedly covered what they billed as the 'dust-up in the powder room', one of the apparently innumerable 'rows in the ladies' toilets at the Barrowland'. An argument had broken out between two teenage girls. When another woman had stepped in to defuse the situation, one of the teenagers had swung a stiletto. The steel-tipped spike bit deeply into the would-be peacemaker's head, sparking a mass brawl. Though the violence itself was unremarkable, the assailant's age wasn't. When the 17-year-old went up before the Sheriff Court, he told the teenager how fortunate she was not to receive a prison sentence, before placing her on two years' probation.

For many, the Barrowland's struggles seemed to reflect a wider truth about a city that had begun to slide into hard, dangerous times. For many it seemed as if violence, an ever-more severe and apparently unavoidable violence, was becoming an increasing fact of life. That is certainly the impression that could have formed for regular readers of the city's tabloid press. These were fruitful years for its legion of crime correspondents. Some were, if not household names, then at the very least storied members of Glasgow's press clubs and drinking dens. Men like Arnot McWhinnie, the *Daily Record*'s chief crime reporter. The *Daily Record* in particular knew precisely the crimes its audience wanted to devour. Corruption often did well. On 16 February 1968, the paper led with a bold story on the lawyer of three convicted gangsters, who had himself been handed down an eight-year sentence. A black-and-white photo of James Latta – balding, late-forties, softly quivering chin – stares balefully out of the front page, Latta having been convicted of helping his clients, led by the lantern-jawed Frank 'Tarzan' Wilson, plot to have two of their criminal associates sprung from prison. The editorial marvels at 'the first major success of the campaign of a city's dedicated cops to end an era of fear and intimidation'. After the trial, one of the most senior police figures in Scotland, Detective Superintendent Tom Goodall, the head of Glasgow CID, told the assembled reporters of his delight. His men, he said, had done a very fine job penetrating a gang who had caused havoc across the inner city. The disgraced lawyer's wife is tucked away into the bottom corner of page 19. Eight years is a long time, she explains, but she was planning to stand by him no matter what. If her Jimmy had any fault at all, it was simply that he was too dedicated to his profession.

If unscrupulous lawyers were popular, then murder was something else entirely. The front pages early that year were covered in it: from the killing of a Californian tourist in a campsite outside Edinburgh to the body of a middle-aged woman discovered deep underneath a building site in Liverpool. A 15-year-old girl had been killed in South Lanarkshire. Linda Peacock's body had been dumped in a cemetery. A local labourer was put on trial and quickly found guilty. The *Daily Record* was particularly taken with the first crime: 19-year-old Anita Harris's body had been discovered by a group of schoolboys three weeks after she had been killed. Barry Ashington, a 25-year-old chef from Brighton, was later put on trial, where he pleaded insanity. The court heard dark, unsettling testimony about illicit drugs at the campsite and a strange, bearded man with a 'hippie bell' tied around his neck. Of particular interest was the small and apparently insignificant detail of a crucifix that had been discovered near the body, along with a packet of birth control pills and a CND badge, and a scrap of paper with an address written on it. The trial ground on and the dead woman's smiling face continued to take up the front pages, contrasted jarringly with coverage of The Beatles' increasingly chaotic spiritual pilgrimage to India.

Gangs were also a popular topic, though coverage was beginning to gravitate towards Glasgow's organized criminal underworld. Stories of sinister figures like John 'The Fishman' Gorevan and John 'Bandit' Rooney dominated the inside pages, along with the brilliant, indefatigable detectives tasked with stopping them, characterized in breathless *Boys Own* prose ('Detective Sergeant Jack Beattie ... the underworld knows him as 'the Flash'). These pieces also carried helpful explainers of the slang and shorthands increasingly exported from the language of American organized crime. Omertà ('the words that means silence') and racketeering were things one could read about from the safety of the kitchen table, in Dennistoun or Cathcart, from Tradeston to Hyndland.

Towards the end of the decade, the papers began to reflect a growing concern linked to groups of disaffected and mostly disorganized gangs of young men from the most deprived and isolated corners of the city, including the still-novel high-rise blocks of flats that had begun to dominate the cityscape during the 1960s. They were the successors to the famed and feared 'razor gangs' of the Twenties and Thirties, so memorably documented in H. Kingsley Long's novel *No Mean City*. In 1968, the English crooner Frankie Vaughan had made his way to Easterhouse, one of the increasingly notorious housing schemes on the eastern fringes of the city. The area had been struggling under the weight of violence shared out between the Drummie, Pak, Rebel and Toi gangs. Slashings and stabbings were an increasingly common fact of life. Vaughan gave an impassioned speech flecked with earnestly applied 1960s slang, calling for his audience to lay down their weapons. 'There's no more gangs. There's no more Drummie, OK? It's out.' But any real progress was illusory, despite the rapturous applause caught by the assembled press.

An ITV documentary shot the same year opens with several young children sitting along a wall daubed in graffiti. GET TO FUCK FRANKIE VAUGHAN WE'LL KEEP OUR CHIBS* is the message, daubed in bold block chalk. *The Gangs of Glasgow* documents an afternoon in the life of the Shamrock Gang as they spend the day aimlessly flitting around the city centre. The voiceover bemoans how in a city of over one million people, a

---

* Glaswegian slang for knives or homemade shanks.

minority still practise 'explosive violence for kicks'. Joe Devlin is introduced to the viewer as the 16-year-old leader of the gang, responsible for all kinds of mayhem and destruction. The viewer is presented with a bleary eyed, puffy cheeked boy with vivid red hair and full, almost purple lips. He is given a chance to explain himself in a disconcertingly soft, shyly gentle voice. He'd already served time in a young offenders' institute, but then so had most of his peers. What separated him from the pack was a willingness to do what others wouldn't. It was easy for him to lead, Devlin explains. 'I'm always at the front. Everyone wants to be ... but I am. If there's any damage, if there's a fight.' The interviewer wants to know whether they fight with their fists, and doesn't hold back on the incredulity when informed that they don't. Instead, it's hatchets, knives, or whatever other weapon they can get their hands on. The unseen interviewer wonders whether they aren't worried they could kill someone. Devlin explains that murder isn't something that's at the forefront of his mind, not in the middle of battle. 'You don't think you're going to kill him. [Even] when six of you plunge him at the same time. He might be seriously ill but you don't think you're going to do him in,' he adds with a slight shrug. It has, he admits, happened a couple of times, though these things didn't ever sit too heavily on his conscience.

In fact, he still sleeps as soundly as on any other night, he explains with deadpan teenage bravado.

The dancehalls weren't immune from these concerns. In 1966, a 23-year-old teacher at a Glaswegian Approved School for delinquent boys went 'undercover' in a Maryhill gang. Writing under the name James Patrick, the resulting book, *A Glasgow Gang Observed*, became an instant classic of popular sociology on publication in 1973. Patrick documented his four months with the Young Team in granular detail, including the pitched battles and the boys often violent sexual conquests in communal stairwells and closes around their 'territory'. It presents a stark portrait of the boys' sheer social alienation and poverty, as well as the heavy-handed, often brutally violent, police response. After one particularly bloody encounter in a Maryhill pub, the boys make their way into the city centre for a night at the Granada dancehall. After a brief lull, normal order is resumed. Patrick describes an atmosphere of barely repressed malice and sexual tension on the dancefloor. The girls are described as 'looking superb in the half light, their very young faces painted and their eyes black with mascara ... in the corner of the room, in the corridors, and even on the steps ... there is some fierce "winchin" (kissing) in progress.'

The brawl starts when one of 'the team' – a diminutive boy also named Patrick – approaches a group of men, before being attacked and badly beaten. The bouncers arrive to provide a further beating until blood streams from the boy's mouth and a flurry of excited, vicious kicks sends his prone body spinning further and further towards the main door. The band plays on as normal – 'Reach Out' by the Four Tops – until the violence ends as quickly as it had erupted. Suddenly, the largest of the bouncers returns to the dancefloor with blood stains seeping into his frilly white dress shirt. The author makes a quiet exit and waits for his stricken comrade outside, but leaves when it's apparent that he isn't going to appear.

For many, there was the conscious sense of living through history, trapped tight in a period of rapid and disquieting change. This wasn't just some vague, retroactively diagnosed cultural shift, or generational conflict. This was something physical. Something solid and real and entirely unignorable. So much has been written about the history of Glasgow's built environment in the twentieth century that it can be difficult to disentangle myth from reality. By the late 1940s, the city's housing stock was crumbling, with over a third of the total dwellings in the city barely fit for human habitation, or on structural life support. This was an era of indefatigable city elders and visionary planners, who saw the possibility of a bold and unprecedented new future seeded in the misery of the present. The past was no good and had to be dispensed with. At least, that's how the history is often told, though the truth was, and remains, much more complex than that.

Between 1951 and 1971, Glasgow's population had dipped from over a million to around 870,000. The New Towns had begun to spring up, first in East Kilbride and Glenrothes, followed by Cumbernaud and the others. By 1968, some of Glasgow had taken on a left-behind feeling. The familiar images and explanations. Economic downturns and heavy industry evaporating. Demolition was a common sight, though it wasn't always carried out with the utmost efficiency. Half-obliterated tenement buildings were a fact of life around the city, while urban planners rubbed their hands together and laid down strips of motorway that pulverized once historic areas to dust and cut the city into apparently arbitrary chunks. The trams had long been ripped out and the high-rises were springing up with cheerful abandon, at every point of the compass. The famous names that barely lasted forty years before coming down themselves. Red Road, Bluevale and Whitevale Towers in Dennistoun, and Hutchesontown C and E down in the Gorbals (the first of these better known as simply 'Hutchie C', or 'The Hanging Gardens of the Gorbals' for those of a more poetic persuasion). There were plenty of smaller developments which never quite gathered the same renown or column inches, and nothing like the later infamy.

Today, there are plenty who still push the idea that the past simply disappeared on contact with modernity. But that was never quite the whole story. The thousands who moved to their new homes in the sky didn't become foreigners to their own city overnight. They still had the same fears and concerns. The same weekend desires and snatched freedoms. To some extent, life went on perhaps much as it ever did, even if the backdrop had been rebuilt into unfamiliarity.

If no one was expecting utopia, there might be the reasonable hope of improvement. But even these modest dreams weren't so easy to grasp or hold tight. On 16 August 1969, an article ran on page 7 of the Saturday edition of the *Daily Record*. Most of the 150 families who had moved into the towering new Glasgow Corporation flats in Whitevale Street, Dennistoun, had been looking forward to the promised luxuries of spacious bedrooms and mixer taps, and purpose-built balconies with crystal-clear views of the city and beyond. But there had been a problem, right from when the very first flats had been let that May.

The nearby chemical factory would belch fumes into the residents' flats, day and night. The local SNP councillor is quoted lambasting a series of desperate planning errors, though the Corporation Housing Department was quick to interject that it was all part of the master plan. In fact, its extensive research had shown that smoke would only be carried into the flats around twenty-two times a year. An elderly couple stare back from a quarter-page black-and-white photograph, from their balcony on the twelfth floor. It was hard to keep the windows clean for long, the woman explained to the paper's reporter. And the smell was something else. Something terrible, especially on the weekends.

PATRICIA DOCKER

As with any other origin story, it's best to begin with what are generally accepted as the facts: the verifiable details that anchor myth to reality. It begins with a woman at home, preparing for a night out. Twenty-five-year-old Patricia Docker lived with her parents and four-year-old son, Sandy, down in the red-brick respectability of Battlefield, then as now a solid outpost in Glasgow's Southside. Her work as a nursing auxiliary at Mearnskirk Hospital, right down in Newton Mearns on the outer southern fringes of the city, ran to a well-worn routine. Night shifts from 10 p.m. to 8 a.m., with a few days off peppered across the week. Few accounts fail to mention her looks. She was pretty, they say, before offering a perfunctory missing-person's-appeal-worth of supplementary detail. Medium height, slim build, hazel eyes and wavy brown hair cut into a bob. For the writers that can't resist an extra burst of feeling, she is described as an angel. The angelic nurse, living with her child in a suburban idyll.

In 1963, Patricia had married a soldier named Alex Docker and the couple later made the move to RAF Digby in Lincolnshire, one of the oldest air force bases in the country. The marriage was an unhappy one almost from the start and the relationship had soon begun to fray so far from home. The prospect of divorce was raised more than once and by 1968, Patricia had made the decision to move back to Glasgow with their young child. By this time, Alex had risen to the rank of corporal and decided to stay in England, rather than return north. In truth, not much else has survived of their life together. No one thought to record precisely what kind of marriage it was, or what form their unhappiness began to take. But the move home made sense. Patricia Docker had a toddler to raise and parents who could help her. Space, as so many have written since, to break off into a new chapter of her life.

February 1968 was unusually cold, even by the typical standards of a Glaswegian winter. Thursday 22nd marked a day off for Patricia and the opportunity of a night out. The Majestic Ballroom on Hope Street had been a wildly popular addition to the city centre's nightlife, ever since its conversion in 1958 from the bones of the grandly modernist Savoy Theatre, designed at the start of the century by James Miller, one of the city's most decorated architects. The clientele was, for dancehall standards, stolidly respectable. A place where the fun only ever went so far, at least by reputation. This is where Patricia Docker told her parents she was heading, to meet friends for a night at the dancing. But that wasn't how the evening developed. Instead, she was to make her way to the Barrowland, for the Over-25s, more commonly and unkindly known as the 'Grab-a-Granny night'.

Most reports acknowledge that Patricia Docker's motives for obscuring her own tracks are permanently lost to the past. But those Thursday nights at The Barrowland Ballroom were notorious, in their own way. People

Patricia Docker

knew what went on there, the kind of permissiveness that the Over-25s night represented. It isn't difficult to imagine a young woman who would rather her parents didn't know where she was headed. Only later did this apparently small, everyday falsehood take on a heightened significance. Patricia Docker had left her parents' flat in Battlefield dressed in a yellow crocheted mini dress, topped with a grey, blue-collared duffle coat. She wore brown heels with a matching handbag. At least these are the details that have been handed down across the decades.

No one can say now with any certainty what time she arrived at the Barrowland, or detail the precise story of how her night, or even much of its aftermath, unfolded. Subsequent accounts have rarely been able to resist a string of novelistic flourishes, as if the facts of the story alone don't have the required muscle and heft to support themselves. As if the reader can't be trusted to keep focus without the additional brightly daubed fictional colour. They have Patricia Docker heading to the ladies' toilets on arrival to check on her make-up and smooth down her outfit before breathlessly disappearing into the crush of expectant bodies on the dancefloor. They take her to the bar, away from the worst of the smoke and noise, before settling into position overlooking the action. Alone and quietly observant, until the man arrives at her side. In some tellings he stands unobtrusively, before pulling into focus with a smile, which is shyly reciprocated. It depends on the writer, on how far exactly they're willing to push things. Some are more creative than others. It is a tempting scene to dramatize, with the possibilities for a segment of pure Glasgwegian noir right there for the taking. Perhaps Patricia Docker stumbles slightly and the two gently collide. Not too much detail of this apparition's appearance is ever given. That will come later. On the night of his first appearance, some concessions are made to the dark, some recognition given to the limits of tasteful speculation. The man is given good manners. He listens attentively, straining slightly to hear against the music. They begin to dance under the lights. For the next few hours, he will be her life.

Here this invented scene cuts to black. Early the next morning, 67-year-old Maurice Goodman left his Southside home in the weak winter light. Goodman lived at 27 Carmichael Place in Battlefield, a short walk from where he kept his car in a garage on nearby Carmichael Lane. A thick frost had formed overnight, coating the suburban streets and the thin cobbled approach to the lane. Within a few steps, Goodman came across a figure, naked and inert, spread across the entrance to his lock-up. A woman's body, lying on the frozen ground. Maurice Goodman's role in this story is brief, a walk-on part with only the scantest dialogue. He could instantly tell what he was dealing with, he later told reporters. Yes, she was frozen, he said, 'like brushing against a block of ice'. In his initial call to the police, a panicked Goodman incorrectly identified the body as male. The immediate official response was slow, almost leisurely. There was no reason yet to label the death suspicious and it was likely assumed that the body was that of an unfortunate vagrant, or a drunk who hadn't quite made it home from the night's excesses. To die without dignity wasn't unheard of. In fact, it seemed to be occurring on an almost daily basis.

Two traffic police were the first to arrive, followed just after 8 a.m. by Detective Constable Norman MacDonald and Detective Sergeant Andrew Johnstone. Having parked at the Overdale Street end of the lane, they walked to the garage. It didn't take long to establish that this was more than a grim accident. That this was a murder scene. The woman was lying on her back, with her head turned to her right. Her clothes were gone, save for a shoe found nearby (some writers round it up to a pair) and it was clear she had been beaten.

The two detectives called for a police pathologist, Dr James Imrie, to establish a cause and time of death. He noted that rigor mortis had already set in, confirming that the woman had been dead for several hours, though the cold made it impossible to be any more precise.

Ligature marks were discovered around her neck, with vivid bruises that suggested strangulation, though no murder weapon was found on or near the body. Some urgency was belatedly established. The alley and surrounding streets began to fill with a rapidly multiplying hive of detectives and early, eager crime reporters. Identification of the body was still some time off. This is just how things worked then. Occasionally you got lucky and often you didn't. The victim didn't appear to have a handbag, or anything that might speak to who she was, or had been.

The crime scene – that's what the lane had become by now – became increasingly overcrowded. It wasn't simply that the detectives present were ignorant of how to preserve it, just that the day had imperceptibly already begun to take on a momentum of its own, apparently quite outside any one person's control. Imrie would have gone about his work briskly, taking the body's temperature and gathering hair samples. A black-and-white photo from that morning shows a cluster of men in heavy overcoats and pork pie hats erecting the portable police tent that had been called into Carmichael Lane. So many boots in the frame, scuffing at the icy ground, lapping at the edges of the freshly locked-down crime scene. Another shows a procession of plain-clothes detectives making their way down the lane, crammed shoulder to shoulder, led by Detective Superintendent Elphinstone Dalglish, easily distinguishable by his white mackintosh – the rest of the men are clad in muted black and grey – and thick-rimmed glasses. The most detailed testimony from that morning comes from Joe Jackson, then a young Detective Constable working in Glasgow's Northern Division. In his 2008 memoir *Chasing Killers*, he describes rushing to the scene after the call went out to every available unit in the city. It wasn't like today, he writes. Less rigid, perhaps. Certainly less meticulous. There is a halfway-gentle disdain that cuts through his words on how the crime scene was preserved that morning: 'In those days, it was not appreciated how important it was to preserve the locus in as pristine a condition as possible, so all the flatfoots were allowed to go into the lane and view the body.'

It took two hours for the police to set up door-to-door inquiries. In some accounts, the tabloids get there first, their sharp, ravenous reporters diligently canvassing neighbours and hunting down any stray scraps of detail for their stories, until being warned off by detectives. Police or press, it didn't really matter. The results were the same, a shapeless mush of false starts and dud information. Maurice Goodman still didn't recognize the woman. He was no use to anyone, as if his mind had flown off somewhere else entirely (*'the joiner'* leaves the story forever now, stumbling straight out of frame, stricken and confused). These initial inquiries didn't yield much else. Someone thought they might have heard a brief scuffle in the early hours and a woman's disembodied voice shouting 'leave me alone'. Another neighbour might have seen a figure matching the victim's still-vague description getting into a car, but couldn't be sure in the dark. A journalist had thrown a party in a block of flats the next street over, though none of the stream of guests who had come and gone during the night had seen anything suspicious, or anything much at all.

By the afternoon, the body had been taken to the police mortuary for a postmortem. It confirmed strangulation as the cause of death and that the woman had been menstruating. A search of the lane had turned up a used sanitary towel, though still nothing in the way of clothes or belongings. These details were to matter later, far more than anyone could have reasonably predicted. News of the unidentified body began to spread around the Southside. The commotion had the locals excited. It got people talking. The half-frozen body, found in Carmichael Lane. The naked woman found in the weak morning light. The news was to make the evening papers. Another murder. A woman killed. The news spread city wide, carried into kitchens and living rooms on a bed of rough newsprint. Sometime in the afternoon, nurses from the nearby Victoria Infirmary had arrived to try and help with identification. They peered closely at the body, but nothing came to them. The woman's face was too badly damaged.

That evening, 63-year-old John Wilson read about the nameless body found a few streets down from his family's home on Langside Place. Patricia Docker's father had become increasingly worried when his daughter had failed to return home after her night dancing at the Majestic. That morning, he and his wife, Pauline, had shrugged it off. They thought Patricia might have stayed the night with a friend, or with colleagues from her work. It wouldn't have been the first time. The Majestic was a way off in the city centre. Safer, perhaps, than risking the journey home in such bitter conditions. But it was unlike their daughter at least not to phone. Things unravelled rapidly from here, with each step of the sequence running remorselessly into the next. John Wilson took himself down to the nearest police station, with a recent picture of Patricia ('armed' with a picture of his daughter, as one true crime blog has it, as if it were a weapon burrowed into the lining of his winter coat). At the mortuary, it didn't take long for the father to identify his daughter. Patricia Docker had been killed. Found naked, half frozen, in a lane minutes from her home.

The front page of the next morning's *Daily Record* led with her photo, a black-and-white image of the dead

woman smiling out under the headline MURDER RIDDLE
OF NURSE PATRICIA, opposite a quarter-page advert for
Eldorado, 'Scotland's best-selling proprietary wine (you
can TASTE the strength in every bottle)'. Elphinstone
Dalglish provided a few brisk quotes for the piece. 'We
are treating this as a murder. She had a wedding ring on
the third finger of her right hand.' If anyone, anyone at
all, had any information then they were urged to come
forward. The same paper soon carried another, even
starker cover. MURDER ... DID YOU SEE HER? MRS PATRICIA
DOCKER, FOUND MURDERED NEAR CARMICHAEL PLACE,
LANGSIDE, GLASGOW, ON FEBRUARY 23. The head of CID,
Tom Goodall, made a plea for the friends she'd been out
with to get in touch. Patricia Docker's clothes were still
missing. John Wilson is quoted briefly, as is Pauline. She
gave reporters a few words ('I'll have to look after my
grandson Sandy') and is identified as a nurse, just like her
daughter.

Patricia Docker didn't hold the front pages for too
long. Over the following days, her murder found itself
slipping further into the paper, boxed in and squeezed
into ever smaller paragraphs. An accidental fire down
south at a psychiatric hospital in Shropshire had killed
twenty-four patients, relegating the local Southside killing to the inner pages. As usual, no shortage of ugliness
and few apparent limits to despair. Further killings,

maimings and corruption, covered from every corner of the nation and beyond. The world so full of horrors, day after day. Naturally the most titillating updates, as and when they came, boosted the murder of 'the nurse' back into prominence. Police frogmen dredged the River Cart, near where Patricia Docker's body had been discovered. Her handbag was pulled out, along with the casing for her watch. Images survive of the search, with stout men in regulation wetsuits on their hands and knees, or else waist deep in the freezing sludgy water. On 26 February, Elphinstone Dalglish made two new appeals to the public. They wanted to speak with the driver of a Morris 100 Traveller, which had stopped in Langside Avenue at the entrance to Queen's Park late on Thursday 22nd. A young woman had climbed into the passenger seat and the car had last been seen heading east towards the Langside monument. The two were never traced. There also was the white Ford Consul, which had been spotted turning into Overdale Street at 11.30 p.m. the same night. A man and woman, driver and passenger, in the car, which had crawled slowly across the streets around Carmichael Lane. In one news article, a policewoman is pictured in a 'mock-up' (these techniques still carried a buoyant novelty to them, the prim quotation marks are the paper's own) of what the victim would have looked like on her night out at the dancing. The model is dressed in the same clothes as the dead woman, though her face is erased into an eerie, permanent blankness.

The main focus was on the Majestic, where it was still believed Patricia Docker had spent her last hours. Police had visited the ballroom on the 23rd, canvassing dancers and interviewing management, but few seemed able – or willing – to give up much in the way of useful information. Dalglish appeared in the *Daily Record* again, appealing for the hoped-for witnesses to do the right thing. 'We are sure that many people who were at the Majestic are scared to come to us because they had not told their wives or husbands where they were going. Their confidence will be respected.' One dancer from the Majestic did come forward and insisted that he'd danced with the victim, though his claim was comprehensively disproved. Murder can make people say and do all sorts of irregular things. Whatever might get them closer to the action, closer to the centre of something bigger than themselves. These false starts carried heavy consequences for the investigation. By the time a more reliable inform-ant came forward to confirm that Patricia Docker had instead been at The Barrowland Ballroom, her murder had already begun to ebb from the news. Momentum was squandered. According to Joe Jackson, the team of detec-tives on the case had been putting in fourteen-hour days, reporting to the same Southside murder caravan at 8 a.m.

to work straight through until their shift ended at 10 p.m. This pace and intensity didn't, couldn't, last. One morning, they'd arrived to find the caravan gone. 'Immediately', Jackson writes, 'my thought – and that of every other detective – was that the crime had been solved while we were off duty.' Instead, resources had been diverted to the scene of two fresher killings. An elderly couple had been stabbed to death in their flat, in a high-rise block out west in Cardonald. The area was covered by the Govan Station, who were already dealing with another separate open murder file. The same man, a fruit-shop owner from Govan, was eventually convicted for all three killings.

Patricia Docker, 'the nurse', was to be left to the attention of local Southside detectives. If dancers at the Majestic had been cautious with their recollections, then the Barrowland clientele were something else again. Few wanted to admit to being present on the Thursday night the nurse had been killed. Silence meant self-preservation. It meant protection from the lies you might have told, about where you'd been and who you'd been with. It quickly became apparent that those Thursday nights at the Barrowland were populated by a cast of well-dressed ghosts. The weekly churn of hundreds of men and women who were never really there, at least not as their daytime apparitions. To break the silence meant opening yourself up to all kinds of unwanted scrutiny. It meant to willingly place your life under the beam of an ugly, vivid spotlight, centred straight on all the things you might rather remain forgotten. A fumble. A tipsy lumber with another anonymous dancer was one thing. But this was murder. A woman killed. For every crank and oddball – like the strident dancer from the Majestic who was so convinced he'd danced with Patricia Docker – there were many more who didn't want to get mixed up with something of such obvious seriousness.

For many, the police's earnest public promises of anonymity didn't really count for much. Weeks bled into months. Nothing moved, despite the man hours, despite the public appeals. No witnesses or suspects; not even a credible body of evidence. Alex Docker, Patricia's estranged husband, had been interviewed right at the very beginning of the investigation. Then, as now, it was the very first place detectives were likely to look. If little is known about Patricia Docker, then even less is known of her husband. He arrives briefly into the picture, to formally identify the body as well as to provide a watertight alibi (though on leave in Scotland, he'd been at his parents' house in East Lothian before making his way to St Andrews). There wasn't too much else to say, he explained to the police, seeing that he hadn't seen his wife for around five months, give or take. As the months passed and press interest receded, life in Glasgow carried on along the same well-worn grooves. Dancers packed the Barrowland and Celtic followed their 1967 European Cup triumph with a clean sweep of domestic trophies. The freshest high-rise developments began to fill with eager, optimistic residents moving into these bold new symbols of the city's future. New murders filled the tabloids. Fresher killings that relegated Patricia Docker to an apparently permanent obscurity. It wasn't apathy exactly. Without a suspect, without even a reliable description, it was impossible to know who or what you were meant to be searching for. To the detectives tasked with solving her killing, Patricia Docker became an open file, an unsolved case. But that was never all she was.

In 2008, forty years after his mother's murder, Sandy Docker spoke to the *Daily Record* in his first ever interview, splashed out across the front page. At 44, he was a middle-aged man himself by then, living in the south of England. 'When I see a picture of Pat Docker on the television screen or in a newspaper, there is the four-year-old part of me that recognises the lady as my mother but the rational me, the adult, sees her in a more detached way', he told reporters at the tabloid. His father had remarried, and his new wife had raised Sandy as her own. There were vague memories of his mother. Walking together in a Glasgow park. Little things like that. He was sorry, so sorry, that her life had ended the way it had, barely into her twenties. But he couldn't say he'd suffered, at least 'not in a tangible way. Who knows what it would have been like if she hadn't died?'

* * *

It's a freezing cold afternoon in early December 2021 and I'm mindlessly watching the midday rain batter off the concrete in the square outside Peckham Library, a mile or so from my home in south-east London. Inside, the heating has been cranked up high and I'm starting to get drowsy. For the last hour or so, I've been at my desk reading and rereading through the set of disorganized tabs on my laptop. They range from bluntly composed news stories, old and contemporary, to the relentless minute-by-minute churn of various social media platforms. On Facebook, I scroll down a list of names that had sprung up in an earlier search. The screen shows a row of late-middle-aged men living in England, each named Alex Docker. There's a couple of them who could feasibly be the man whose mother was murdered in February 1968 after a night dancing at The Barrowland Ballroom and I click into their profiles to see if there's any stray detail that might reveal the identity of the man I'm looking for. I think about sending the men a message and wonder exactly what it would say and how I might introduce myself. Should I go for the resolutely formal, clipped professional greeting, or the more detailed, reassuringly friendly and open-handed line of enquiry? Nothing feels right, or good. And, assuming I discover which one is Patricia Docker's son, what exactly would I be looking for him to say that he hasn't said before?

Do I want him to repeat how he was sorry that his mother was murdered before he had a chance to know her? Or am I supposed to try and wheedle out a new line, some fresh quotes about grief and loss, and anger? I close the page and retreat back to the comfortingly granular digital newsprint on the next page.

JEMIMA MACDONALD

The second woman's body was discovered in a derelict tenement building in Bridgeton on the morning of Monday, 18 August 1969, just under a mile from the Barrowland. She was dressed in a black pinafore dress, with a white blouse and sling-back high-heel shoes. There had been whispers in the neighbourhood after a group of children had been overheard the day before talking between themselves about 'a body in the building'. But whispers were all they'd remained at first. It had been a notably hot summer and the children's chatter was initially dismissed as the product of their overheated imaginations.

Bridgeton was going through a difficult period, though there were some that thought its foreboding reputation to be slightly outsized. Whatever the precise truth, there was no shortage of 'condemned' blocks waiting their turn for demolition in the inner East End. Their presence loomed heavy, freighted with danger and sadness. Most

Jemima MacDonald

people did their best to avoid these gloomy, terminal spaces, at least if they could help it. Everyone apart from the morbidly curious, the daredevil young, or those harbouring their own specific, and perhaps unsayable, motives.

Thirty-two-year-old Jemima MacDonald lived at 15 Mackeith Street, twenty yards from the derelict building where her body was later found. Born in 1937, she was one of seven children raised across Glasgow. Not much is known about her early years, though there are a few flashes of detail, most of them sketching the picture of a difficult youth. Mima, as she was known, is defined in several reports as being constantly 'unlucky' with the men in her life, having suffered repeated bouts of domestic violence across several relationships. But her brief, incomplete biography isn't a story of unrelenting grimness. She was well known in Bridgeton as a cheerful presence around the area, whether running errands on the local high street or stopping for a chat and a drink at one of its cafes.

By 1969, she was a single mother-of-three, living in the one-room flat on Mackeith Street, with Elizabeth (12), Andrew (9) and Alan (7). Little mention is made of their father in contemporary accounts of their mother's life and MacDonald had her own tightly drawn networks. Her sister, Margaret O'Brien, lived across the landing and would regularly help with childcare when necessary. MacDonald enjoyed her semi-regular forays to the dancing, particularly to the nearby Barrowland. Despite her modest circumstances, there were still opportunities for a life outside the domestic routine. The Barrowland offered escape, however temporary. The space where you could become someone else, if never quite the figure of your wildest, or most cherished dreams.

The evening of Saturday, 16 August had begun like so many others before it. After making dinner for the children, MacDonald had put together her outfit, topped with a brown wool coat and headscarf. After dropping the children at her sister's, she'd walked the twenty minutes or so to the Barras, before settling at Betty's Bar across the road from the Barrowland itself. Several witnesses from the bar later reported seeing her drinking with a handsome, well-dressed young man, aged somewhere between 25 and 35. MacDonald was a fairly well-known face at the dancing, if not quite a regular, though she'd attended the preceding Thursday's 'Over-25s' night. Inside, she was spotted dancing with the same man, who witnesses later described as having shortish, light red hair. She seemed, they said, happy enough in the figure's company.

The details that marked the rest of her night at the Barrowland remain unknown. As with Patricia Docker, this emptiness has served as bait for generations of writers who can't quite restrain themselves from filling in the gaps in the narrative. In their 1998 book *Bible John: Hunt for a Killer*, journalists Alan Crow and Peter Samson have Mima MacDonald heading to 'the ladies' room' on arrival (just as their vision of Patricia Docker had done) to touch up her make-up and pull the rollers from her hair. After this brief interlude, they have her leaving the 'protection' of the bathroom and making her way to the dancefloor ('she'd done it many times before and it always worked'). They have her nodding and smiling through the crowd, weaving between bodies until she makes it back to her companion, the well-dressed figure with the reddish hair and 'gleaming white shirt'. The two begin to dance, talking – the authors imagine – about MacDonald's children, 'but not making a big thing of it'. The handsome, immaculately dressed figure is a case study in evasion. He listens quietly, venturing a few clipped facts from his own life. He is written as a polite, attentive presence, just like Patricia Docker's dancing partner. He speaks clearly, if quietly. In this telling, Mima MacDonald is relaxed. She is happy for the company and confident in the night unfolding around her. After the final note of the final dance, the authors take MacDonald back to the ladies' toilets for a final check of her make-up, before the pair leave the dancehall arm in arm at midnight.

The imagined scene doesn't end at the door of the dancehall. From the Barrowland, they head into Bain Street and down across London Road and on to Bridgeton Cross. Later, there were witnesses to support this, who thought they saw the pair together, walking across into Bridgeton. They make for the abandoned building on Mackeith Street ('walking slowly, it should have taken no more than half an hour'). They arrive at the dilapidated tenement ('an ideal spot for a quiet session of kissing, cuddling and heavy petting'). It's only here that the authors leave us, tactfully stopping just short of the door of the empty ground-floor flat.

Margaret O'Brien wasn't immediately concerned when her sister still hadn't appeared the next morning. It wasn't unusual for her to sleep in after a Saturday night at the dancing. O'Brien went about her usual routine and getting the children organized. As the hours passed, the worry began to ratchet up. Sunday passed by, with no sign of her sister. By Monday morning, O'Brien asked her neighbours – known to be regulars at the Barrowland – whether they'd seen or heard anything. On leaving the flat around 10 a.m., she'd encountered another group of children, chattering about the body over the road, in the abandoned tenement. After walking the twenty or so yards, she'd arrived in the close. It was here that she discovered her sister's partly clothed body, dumped in a bed-recess.

The news travelled quickly and, before long, the building and its surrounds were covered with curious, horrified spectators from the area. One account suggests that the body was moved before detectives – again led by Detective Chief Superintendent Tom Goodall – made it to the scene, potentially destroying crucial physical evidence. The facts of the violence were plain enough. Mima MacDonald had been badly beaten and strangled with her own tights. She had, like Patricia Docker, been menstruating. And like Docker, her handbag was missing.

The killing made page 11 of the next day's *Daily Record*, while the front page led with a report of the deepening crisis in Northern Ireland as the IRA demanded the immediate disbandment of the quasi-military 'B-Specials' police force (rendered in tabloidese as WE'LL SHOOT BRITISH – WARNS IRA). Mima MacDonald is given a few paragraphs under the 'Record Reporter' byline, set down underneath the headline WOMAN'S MIDNIGHT WALK ENDED IN MURDER.

There is a helpfully illustrated photo of the entrance to the Mackeith Street tenement building (or 'Death Street', as it had been rechristened by the paper). It shows a cluster of cars lined up the street and a few austere civilians passing by. On the extreme right of the frame is a trio of small children dressed in white (one can't help but wonder if these are perhaps the same nameless children who discovered the body). There are neat, almost cartoonish little diagrams pointing to the 'dead woman's home' and the 'block where the body lay'. A quarter-page photo of a detective studying a clipboard dominates the bottom of the page. The man clasps the wooden frame with a pipe dangling from his mouth and a chequered deerstalker covering his head, cast as the very image of reassuring expertise. Pasted into the corner of the same image is a small picture of Mima MacDonald. It isn't the clearest photo. Her face is angled to the left and her eyes are closed, squinting against the sun. DCS Goodall is quoted in the piece again, saying much the same words that were reported in the initial reports of Patricia Docker's killing. 'We are treating this as a case of murder, and we are appealing to anyone with information to come forward.' They specifically wanted to speak with any dancers who'd been at the Barrowland that Saturday night, whether or not they had 'seen the dead girl'.

The appeal provoked a respectable stream of information, some of it useful. A Detective Inspector praised the efforts in the following day's paper, in a short bulletin. Police photographers had arrived at the Barrowland to photograph the crowds, before broadcasting a description of the man Mima MacDonald had been seen with via the venue's sound system. Detectives began to swarm into Bridgeton, pulling statements and quizzing locals. One witness reported seeing MacDonald talking to a man outside 23 Mackeith Street around 12.40 a.m. The wasteland around the tenement was pored over repeatedly without turning up any sign of her missing handbag. Then there was the description of the suspect: 25–35 years old, six foot tall or thereabouts, slim with thin, slightly wan features and reddish hair. The figure was starting to take shape. He might have been wearing a blue suit with a white shirt and tie. But the man had vanished, as if he'd never really existed at all.

Someone came forward to tell detectives they'd seen a couple at the Abercromby Street junction with London Road around 12.15 a.m. In a piece titled THE RIDDLE OF MIMA'S LAST DANCE, Tom Goodall is quoted explaining how there was a growing confidence that they'd successfully pieced together the last moments of 'the mother of three'. Despite 'the reconstruction' they were still 'anxious for public assistance'. Detectives were now comfortable enough, he said, to indulge in some speculation. They felt 'she may have been in the derelict close with a man kissing and cuddling for a while before she was murdered'. The next day saw the publication of TWO PICTURES THAT COULD CATCH A KILLER, under a generic byline. Two full-length photos of Mima MacDonald accompany the piece. She's dressed in the same outfit she'd worn the previous Saturday, a black pinafore dress with a white shirt. It's a better picture than the first rushed offering, the day after her body was discovered. She is offering a gentle, slightly ironic smile at the unseen photographer. The article carried an explanation of the 'death walk' the police are about to stage, with a policewoman dressing in the same clothes to retrace the route from the Barrowland to Mackeith Street. It is hoped, they explained, that the undertaking might somehow serve to 'jog somebody's memory – and provide a clue to the killer'. Naturally, any information, any information at all, would be treated in the very strictest confidence.

By 25 August, connections were starting to be made between the Mima MacDonald murder and other high-profile unsolved killings of women across Scotland, though no one yet was seriously suggesting a single figure might be responsible for this or that specific combination of them. That day's *Daily Record* carried a puff piece by a reporter named Ian Walker. Titled THE KILLER FILES THAT NEVER CLOSE it is, in reality, a laudatory profile of Glasgow's hard-bitten Murder Squad and its 'limitless, detailed and inexhaustible patience'. The focus, when it isn't on the hyper-competent detectives, is trained on five other unsolved killings across Scotland. It mentions Kathleen Veitch, described as 'the spinster' found strangled on the beach at Elie, Fife. There is Catherine Duncan, a 46-year-old housewife from Wallyford, Midlothian, who was killed after a bingo session in February 1968. Following her is 58-year-old Agnes Armstrong, found dead at her home in a Perthshire village in August the same year. There is the 'attractive divorcee' Cathie Maloney who was found strangled in a lover's lane near East Kilbride, only two weeks before Walker's piece appeared. Mima MacDonald and Patricia Docker receive equal weighting and the writer does briefly ask if the cases might be connected. After all, both women had been at The Barrowland Ballroom. Mostly though, the focus alights on the Murder Squad's record. Of the thirty-nine killings in 1967, only one had gone unsolved. Of the forty-one in 1968, that figure sat at three. In 1969 – as of the time the piece was written – it was only two. It is intimated that this is decent-enough cause for confidence in the elite detectives tasked with the most complicated and harrowing investigations. A nameless insider even explains to the reporter that there could never be any question of forgetting the names that remain on the board. He compares it to a jigsaw, where enough study of the general layout might reveal the precise location of the missing piece that will finally give it the correct shape.

These articles couldn't mask the growing desperation and helplessness at the core of the inquiries into Mima MacDonald's murder. That first week, the usual tools had been applied. Detectives began to embark on long, fruitless days of sifting through the available evidence without anything approaching tangible success. After the initial flurry, things had begun to stagnate, just as they had with the Patricia Docker inquiry and all the other unsolved cases that remained pinned up on the Murder Squad's board. It was vowed that this time was going to be different. In late August, a decision was approved at the very highest levels of the Scottish state to try something drastic in an attempt to solve the killing of Mima Mac-Donald, the 'mother-of-three' who had died such a sordid, violent death in the East End. On 26 August, the *Daily Record* published an identikit picture of the figure desperately sought in connection with her murder. Though similar images had been broadcast on Scottish TV, it was the first time such an image had been set down in print in Scotland, after special permission had been granted at the Crown Office in Edinburgh. In the late 1960s, this was still a ground-breaking innovation, despite its sporadic application in print, north and south of the border.

The resultant black-and-white collage put together by a senior lecturer at Glasgow School of Art shows a sinister figure with hooded, narrow eyes baked into a smooth and curiously depthless face. Its lips are thin and pursed and a dark and heavily shaded nose adds to the sense of a scarcely believably human likeness. The hair is swept to the left and its ears protrude cartoonishly. There is the first hint of a double chin, despite the figure's angular face. It is far cruder than the famous image that was to come later. Less vivid or colourful. Less mocking and intense. The accompanying text repeats its dimensions and apparent sartorial choices. The same questions are posed with a new self-assertion, buttressed with the familiar additional bursts of half-speculative detail. Have you seen this man, aged between 25 and 35; between six foot and six foot two; tall; slim build; reddish fair hair cut short; wearing a good blue suit with hand-stitched lapels and a white shirt? The decision had been taken by Tom Goodall, though the head of CID was in no mood to reveal his motives to the press, even if the official stone-walling didn't put an end to the speculation. It was increasingly clear to interested observers that what the police had wasn't nearly enough. Some insiders were worried about the potential legal ramifications of this wildcard flourish. But not Tom Goodall. His confidence wasn't entirely misplaced. In the days following the iden-tikit's publication, there were thousands of responses from all corners of the city. The news desk was inundated with phone calls from people who thought they'd seen the figure, who had information that could crack the case wide open. Calls arrived from England and Ireland, and the furthest reaches of the Scottish Highlands. Another Detective Superintendent, a James Binnie, was wheeled out in front of the tabloids to give a further burst of the same guarded official police-speak. 'Everyone is being checked out ... we are appealing for every dancer who was at the Barrowland that night to come forward. If they are married and out for a night out without their husbands or wives, their confidence will be respected.'

Despite these repeated promises, the same silence persisted. One could pledge the world, but no one could stop
the days drifting into weeks. There were soon other killings to contend with. Just a few days later, the body of a
man in his early twenties was discovered wedged into the
space between two warehouses in the city centre. The
young man had been dead for some time and identification was a struggle. Police believed he might or might not
have been part of a group that had been involved in a
reported warehouse break-in they'd attended a couple of
weeks before. The body had been called in by a pair of
joiners on their way to work. Two men had been appre-
hended for the robbery and were to be kept inside while
detectives probed any possible link to the fresh murder
file. The search for Mima MacDonald's killer carried on,
though police were starting to publicly admit that it was
becoming a long and dispiriting slog. The leads thrown
up by the identikit image were already proving of varia-
ble quality. Though that was to be expected. There was
still much work to do to uncover this strange and nameless murderer's identity. But it was perfectly possible that
the final, crucial clue was right around the corner. At
least, that's how the most reassuring sources put it.

The modern reader would perhaps like to know more
about Mima MacDonald, her life, as well as the circumstances of her murder. One can only reiterate what was

recorded then. Jemima MacDonald was born in 1937 and was one of seven children. She was five foot seven and had shoulder-length dark hair. She lived in Bridgeton and had three children of her own. After her murder, they were immediately taken into care before being raised by their aunt, the woman who found her sister's body in the ground-floor flat of the condemned tenement building.

* * *

More than half a century has passed since Jemima Mac-Donald's murder. It's late April 2022 and I am sitting in a cluttered backroom in the *Daily Record* offices, a low grey building located in a strange and half-finished part of the city centre. It feels like the only fully completed building in the area, aside from a few already battered blocks of newbuild flats, badly stained from the previous winter's rain. There isn't much else to see around here, aside from a few building sites and warehouses. It's just as well, as the room doesn't have a window. The staff have been nothing but patiently helpful as I send ever-more detailed requests for old papers from across the mid-twentieth century. Today I've been reading from the summer of 1969, just before Jemima MacDonald's body was discovered by the children playing in the mid-August sun. It's been a few hours at least, though I'm not exactly sure, having left my phone and laptop in my bag. I turn yellowed page after yellowed page with theatrical carefulness so as not to rip the fragile old newsprint. I wonder how many other people have touched the same musty old paper before me and immediately chastise myself for such self-indulgent wistfulness. The next day I get chatting to the gregarious security guard who lets me in and out of the building. He asks what it is I'm doing cooped up in there, in the airless room with the rows of leather-bound tomes and unwanted office furniture. When I tell him that I'm writing a book about Bible John, he shakes his head and laughs, rubbing his cheek with his hand. After lunch, I find the news article I'd been searching for and feel excitement and maybe something else, like shame, or maybe contentment.

HELEN PUTTOCK

Twenty-nine-year-old Helen Puttock lived with her husband and two young boys at 129 Earl Street, Scotstoun. In late 1969, it was – as it remains to this day – a mostly solidly working-class residential area in Glasgow's western suburbs. On Thursday, 30 October she had made plans to go to the Barrowland with her older sister, Jeannie Williams, who lived a couple of miles further west in Yoker. From their childhood in Partick, the sisters had been close. According to one account, they had rarely if ever fought as young children, and had carried the same easy relationship into adolescence. A picture of cheerful wholesomeness is deftly painted. 'They talked endlessly about boyfriends and their hopes for the future ... and often laughed and joked about the time they worked as "clippies", taking the fares in their uniforms on the buses after leaving school.'

Their parents had divorced when Helen was 18, upon which the sisters were sent to live with their mother, along with their other siblings. Not much is recorded about this time, other than that both finances and family dynamics were often strained. Life changed for Helen – invariably referred to as the 'slim, lovely brunette' – in her early twenties after a spell staying with her brother Sam down in Wokingham, Berkshire. It was there that she met a man named George Puttock. Puttock was a committed young soldier, around the same age as Helen. The courtship was short and intense. By the time Helen returned to Glasgow, the two were engaged. One can refer to Alan Crow and Peter Samson's book for a general overview of the Puttocks' early years together. Living as a soldier's wife wasn't easy, they write, with George often away for weeks on end. Helen spent her days working (it isn't specified at what or where) and long, lonely nights alone in their marital home. Outgoing and intensely social by nature, 'Helen found it hard to cope with her sudden change in lifestyle'. When George was sent on a long-term posting to Germany, Helen decided to follow with their two small children in tow. It was a move that only isolated her further. The tight-knit clique of army wives had no interest in opening their ranks for her. Without any German, life outside the base was equally hemmed in. After a year, Helen communicated that she was moving back to her

Helen Puttock

mother's in Glasgow, though the couple decided to try and make things work long distance.

Life back in Glasgow reverted to moving along well-worn grooves. By the autumn of 1969, that meant a routine of work, childcare and the occasional night at the dancing, accompanied by Jeannie or some friends from the area. According to Crow and Samson, Helen's husband knew that she was going out, 'but what else could he do?' Her letters to Germany suggested a rediscovered sense of herself. That she was enjoying being back in the familiar city, surrounded by familiar support networks.

George Puttock came home as regularly as his leave would allow. Though irregular, their domestic life was, it is intimated, stable enough. Accounts of the early evening of 30 October tend to vary slightly, though they invariably agree that George Puttock wasn't happy about his wife leaving for a Thursday night at the Barrowland, even accompanied by her sister. In an article for the *Scottish Review*, journalist Magnus Linklater quotes him on the 'tremendous fight' between the couple, which eventually ended with his acquiescing and agreeing to serve as babysitter. Crow and Samson outline his objections, which didn't appear to include the Barrowland's particularly seedy reputation. 'To a traditional man', they write, 'brought up in a working class town it wasn't right for a young mum to go out without her husband. But fun loving Helen insisted.'

The sisters got ready at home. Helen changed into a short-sleeved black dress with gold buttons, offset by brown tights and black shoes. Over the top went an imitation ocelot fur coat. Several reports stress how proud she was of it. Jeannie Williams chose a skirt, blouse and a dark green coat with a sheepskin collar. By the end of October, Jemima MacDonald had all but disappeared from the press, though Puttock and Williams would have read about the Bridgeton woman's murder and that of Patricia Docker the year before. There had been a brief dip in the Barrowland's attendances after the late summer news, but months had passed by and the two murdered women had faded from the front pages, despite Jemima MacDonald's sister putting up a £100 reward to try and provoke some renewed public interest. There were fresh killings and scandals to consider, as well as daily life grinding along with the same intensity. Helen and Jeannie's mother had reminded them of the two poor mothers who had been killed, and suggested they stayed home. Linklater's account has Puttock replying dismissively. '"Can you imagine anyone trying anything on me?" she said [showing] her mother her fine, long nails.' Jeannie knew that her sister had a temper. It's true that Helen was always strong, according to her husband. It wasn't uncommon for her to say that she couldn't imagine anyone getting the best of her in a fight.

The sisters set off from 129 Earl Street at 8.30 p.m. and caught a bus on the Dumbarton Road, travelling east to Glasgow Cross, where they arrived around half an hour later. They made their way to the Trader's Tavern on Kent Street, which was already packed with the pre-Barrowland crowd who'd arrived to load up on alcohol before going on to the venue. At the pub, they joined up with their friends Marion Cadder and Jean O'Donnell. With an hour to go before the 10 p.m. closing time, the sisters managed to finish three whiskies each (this point is stressed across several different accounts, as if it's some-how relevant to what was to follow). The group then made the short walk to join the queue, which was already snaking down the Gallowgate.

What happened next that night differs markedly from the stories of Patricia Docker and Jemima MacDonald, even if the ending is the same: the ending that sees a woman killed. There is a simple reason why the weight of available detail is so much heavier here than in the case of the first two murders. There was a witness. The night that unfolded at the Barrowland has been subject to the most careful scrutiny in the decades since, from detectives and journalists to documentary makers and amateur sleuths across Scotland and far beyond. But even these suppos-edly canonical details are more fluid than many have wanted to acknowledge. They come from a single source: Jeannie Williams, Helen Puttock's sister. The patchwork of her reminiscences hasn't stopped writers availing themselves of the chance to stretch out and add a few supplementary details of their own. These lines are still occasionally blurred. Is it Jeannie Williams or is it Alan Crow and Peter Samson speaking in *Bible John: Hunt for a Killer*, when the two women are greeted on entry to the Barrowland (after paying the requisite four shillings) by 'the familiar stench of alcohol and stale cigarette reek [filling] their nostrils as Helen took off her prized coat'?

The Barrowland was predictably packed and the sisters took themselves to Geordie's Byre, the smaller of the venue's two halls, where the house DJs were known to spin records at deafening volume. After half an hour downstairs, they made their way up to the main dancefloor, already filled with couples moving to the live band. In its darkened corners and crevices it was just about possible to momentarily glimpse couples already locked into sloppy, hurried embraces, illuminated by the light thrown off the mirrored ball far up on the ceiling. It was loud, almost deafeningly loud, when Jeannie was approached by a man named John, who struck up a polite, stilted conversation. He told her that he was a builder from Castlemilk, the sprawling housing scheme on the southern outskirts of the city. It was a common joke to witness how often it seemed as if every man at the Barrowland on a Thursday was called John or Jim. From his awkwardness (he stutteringly enquired whether his prospective partner 'came here often'), Jeannie was sure the man was married. The two began to dance and would remain on the dancefloor for the rest of the night.

Helen was soon to find her own partner. There's no way of precisely knowing how it happened. Several accounts embrace the familiar temptation. They have Helen Puttock standing alone, mildly bored and jealous of her sister's easy success. She is set against the heaving dancefloor, caught on the periphery of the noise and excitement. Isolated and alone. The man is leaning against a pillar, not too far away. Jeannie Williams was to catch a good look. He was well dressed in a 'continental' single-breasted suit and leather half boots, which she immediately thought a strange and slightly anachronistic choice. He was around five foot ten, tall and slim, possibly aged around 25–30, with reddish fair hair. Jeannie Williams thought she might have seen the man around before, but there was no way of being sure. He seemed like a man out of place and time. He was polite and well spoken, in a slightly decorous, mannered sort of way with an unmistakably middle-class inflection to his generic West of Scotland accent. Hardly the Barrowland's type, Jeannie Williams was later to recall. He'd approached Helen Puttock and introduced himself – another John – and the two began to dance. The four stuck together closely on the dancefloor, Jeannie and Castlemilk John, with Helen and her John. When the lights came up after the last dance at 11.30 the two men had disappeared to the cloakroom. When they returned, Helen's John had his scarf, which he fussily smoothed down before putting on his coat, which Jeannie Williams thought to be an oddly prissy gesture.

As they made their way towards the cloakroom, she'd decided to get more cigarettes from the machine in the foyer, having doled hers out over the night. But when she pressed the button down for her Embassy Filters, the machine jammed. The reaction from Helen's John was to become an essential part of the night's myth. It was as if something in the man had snapped. He gripped the machine and began to shout. He wanted to see the manager and wouldn't rest until he appeared. The women were embarrassed at the stares from the other couples who were streaming out into the night. But John wouldn't stop shouting until the manager – a squat, muscular man with a scar running down the side of his face – was eventually called to deal with the growing disturbance. John reiterated that they wouldn't be leaving until Jeannie Williams had her money back. Even in the depths of his performative rage, Williams noticed that the man didn't swear. The confrontation didn't really go anywhere. The manager held his ground until suggesting that the irritant might be better taking it up with his assistant downstairs, who was the one in charge of the machines. Before he made for the stairs, John had turned to the group to tell them that this kind of chicanery was to be expected. His father had told him that these places were dens of iniquity, and that the fire that razed the old ballroom to the ground was an inside insurance job.

On his return, John whispered something in Helen's ear. She shook her head slightly and her face briefly changed, though her sister wasn't sure if it was a look of disbelief or something else. He flashed Helen an ID card from his pocket, a gesture she returned with a smile. The foursome spilled out onto the chaos of the Gallowgate, into the bright sickly lights and the crush of couples spreading back out to whatever corner of the city they'd come from and were returning to. At Glasgow Cross, they hailed a cab, though Castlemilk John made his excuses and left to catch a bus from George Square in the city centre. Here, the crudely sketched figure disappears from the picture forever, despite the subsequent urgency of police appeals for him to come forward. The cab drove through Argyle Street and west to Dumbarton Road, past a flurry of billboards (SEX MANIAC SENT TO CARSTAIRS read the headline to the late edition of the *Evening Times*) and the occasional figure prowling the late-night streets on the twenty-minute journey to Scotstoun. The conversation had become clipped and increasingly severe. John was sullen and withdrawn, perhaps at the fact that Jeannie was still with them. The two sisters asked him questions which he scrupulously avoided, though he mentioned that he played golf and that he had a cousin who had recently scored a hole in one. He said something about his sister and immediately backtracked. He seemed to be familiar enough with Glasgow to know about the city bus fares and the Blue Train services that ran north of the

Clyde. He recognized a block of high-rise flats and mentioned his father had once worked in the area.

Then the conversation turned into something else. Something strange and intense. He didn't approve of the married dancers that went to the Barrowland and said something about 'adulterous' women. There was something about the age-old sectarian enmity of Celtic and Rangers. He said he was agnostic, though he knew parts of the Bible by heart. There was a garbled reference to foster homes or foster children and an allusion to Moses and a woman being stoned, or standing at a well. To lighten things, Jeannie asked what he did for Hogmanay. He said he didn't drink, but prayed. Before the taxi pulled into Earl Street, a minor farce played out where John was revealed to have had a packet of cigarettes on him, despite the slightly hysterical performance at the Barrowland. He offered one to Helen, though not Jeannie. He ignored her complaints, though she reached out to grab a handful before he could pull away.

In Scotstoun, John demanded that they drive the extra ten minutes to drop Jeannie off in Yoker. Though uncomfortable, she left the cab at a roundabout at the bottom of her street. Having waved goodbye, she caught a glimpse of her sister and John's impassive face through the car window as it turned back east. It was around half midnight. That wasn't the last sighting that night of the oddly dressed figure from the Barrowland. It was around 2 a.m. when a near-empty night bus travelling along Dumbarton Road picked up a dishevelled figure at the Gardner Street junction. The man's suit was battered and torn, and it appeared as if he'd been rolling in fresh mud. His face was scratched and marked by a vivid red weal. The man disembarked on Gray Street in the city centre, outside the Lorne Hotel on Sauchiehall Street. At least, that's what the majority of subsequent accounts have agreed on. It makes for a powerful final sighting. The muddied, almost vampiric figure stepping off the night bus and straight into the annals of Glaswegian folklore.

Helen Puttock's body was discovered in the pale morning light by a dog walker around 7 a.m., in a back close a few hundred yards from her home at 129 Earl Street. The police and ambulance men had set to work promptly, arriving minutes after the shaken dog walker had called the body in. Helen had been badly beaten and strangled with her own tights. There were signs of a bitter struggle. It looked as if she had tried to escape by clambering up to the railway embankment which ran along the back gardens up from the close. Her fur coat lay nearby, streaked in mud, though some of her other clothes were missing. It was soon established that Puttock – like Patricia Docker and Jemima MacDonald – had been menstruating at the time of her death. Detectives found a used sanitary towel neatly folded and tucked under her armpit. George Puttock had, in one of his own subsequent accounts, spent a sleepless night worrying about his wife's whereabouts. By mid-morning the streets around their home were covered in the usual crush of detectives and the first few reporters who had heard about the murder out west in Scotstoun. On making his way towards the police caravan, George heard a gaggle of bystanders speaking in hushed tones about a woman who had been found dead in the close. At the caravan, he was greeted by a young detective, who immediately vanished to fetch his superior. When he returned, it was with Detective Superintendent Joe Beattie, of the Marine Division based in nearby Partick. Beattie got close to Puttock and asked what his wife had been wearing the night before. When he mentioned the black dress and fur jacket, Beattie stopped him. He was sorry, he told George Puttock. He was sorry, but his wife had been murdered. This brief, dizzyingly direct encounter is by no means the last that we hear from either man.

The next morning's papers carried word of the latest killing, as did the television news, including a report led by a besuited middle-aged news anchor emerging from the shadows of the back court at 95 Earl Street. He explains how the dog walker had found Helen Puttock lying face downwards, her body angled towards a wall. Clothes dance lightly on a washing line behind him as he gestures at the embankment leading to the train lines. In the background squats the dim outline of a high-rise block of flats and some heavy industrial machinery. 'She might at one stage have tried to escape from her attacker,' he says as if commentating on a mediocre afternoon at the racing, 'before being dragged back.'

If the press had previously tentatively linked Patricia Docker and Jemima MacDonald by their mutual association with the Barrowland, then the latest killing offered a fresh opportunity for speculation. The killing appeared on the front page of the *Evening Times*, along with the news of a man charged with murder over the death of an elderly steel worker in Bellshill. The *Daily Record* also put the killing on the front page, along with the news of a hijacked American airliner, which had finally landed at Shannon airport in Ireland after a day-long ordeal. Elphinstone Dalglish had by now taken over from Tom Goodall, who had died suddenly in his late sixties, as the head of Glasgow's CID and is featured in the piece, offering the same old appeals for witnesses to come forward. The first appeal goes out to the cab driver who had picked up the victim and her sister, as well as the potential killer. The second, to the man known only as Castlemilk John. There is a short, helpful account of the previous two murders and a list of the apparently watertight connections between them. 'IT IS KNOWN', the paper barks, that

Helen, her sister and 'a man' had boarded a taxi at Glasgow Cross. 'ALL THREE' of the murdered women had died in a 'similar fashion' and had been 'escorted home' before their deaths. 'ALL THREE' had also had their handbags or purses taken, though no supporting theory was offered yet as to why.

On the next page there is a detailed photo diagram of Earl Street, the newly christened 'Street of Death', just as there had been with Mackeith Street after Jemima MacDonald's murder a few months before. Parked cars line the wide suburban street, though there isn't a single passer-by caught by the camera. Then there are the same helpful bubbles of text, pointing to the precise location of 'the woman found in back court' and the newly set-up police caravan. If anyone had seen 'dark haired Helen' then they were implored to make contact. On Monday, 3 November, the same paper published two full-length photos of the murdered 'mother-of two', dressed in the same clothes she had worn to the Barrowland, caught under the headline HOW HELEN LOOKED THE NIGHT SHE MET A KILLER. It was, the piece admitted, a drastic step to take, although the pictures that had been prepared by 'police photography experts' didn't actually capture Helen Puttock at all, apart from her superimposed head. Instead, the images had been created by dressing an unspecified 'girl' in the murdered woman's clothes.

The precise order of what happened next remains a matter of light conjecture. There is a mostly friendly etymological argument about who it was that came up with the infamous name that was about to be beamed into living rooms and onto news-stands, shop windows and bus stops across the city for the rest of 1969 and beyond. Of who might be able to take credit for conjuring up the image of the folk devil that was about to haunt the city's imagination.

In most accounts, the coinage of 'Bible John' is given as the brilliantly opportunistic work of a star sports reporter at the *Evening Times*, another popular tabloid. When John Quinn died aged 74 in 2011, every glowing obituary in the Scottish press made mention of his manifold virtues. His kindness and fearlessness, as well as his devotion to his craft. Having started at the paper as a news reporter in the early Sixties, he'd worked his way to news editor before a glittering, decades-long stint as a sports reporter, covering Celtic (he had driven to the 1967 European Cup final in Lisbon in a green-and-white hatchback) and boxing ('he could count Sugar Ray Robinson and Muhammad Ali as friends'). In the days following Helen Puttock's murder – the mother-of-two found beaten and strangled in a back close – Quinn had read the drip-fed flow of information on the killer (there was already mention of the figure's apparent penchant for biblical quotation) and decided to give him a name. Bible John stuck immediately. It captured the mood of the killings. The fear and the seediness. The slight and unsaid note of judgement that permeated from the fact that two of the three women had spent their last evenings at the Barrowland's Over-25s night. Every killer needs a name for a chance of enduring notoriety. Glasgow's more astute pressmen knew this, even then. By the autumn of 1969, the freshly christened Zodiac Killer was beginning to haunt Californian imaginations. Another uncaught killer, cloaked in an instantly memorable moniker.

On Tuesday, 4 November even the rival *Daily Record* had to concede to John Quinn's brilliance. DO YOU KNOW BIBLE JOHN? ran alongside the breaking news of a fire that had ripped through the STV studios at the Theatre Royal on Hope Street, which had already killed one of the attending firemen while another had been reported missing at the scene. This report was different from what had gone before regarding any of the prior Barrowland murders. It carried a previously unknown level of detail, as well as much of what had already been broadcast during the still mostly unconnected hunts for Patricia Docker's and Jemima MacDonald's killer. They were looking for a young man named John. Well spoken, well dressed. A young man who goes regularly to the city's Barrowland Ballroom and who may talk of the Bible.

Here was the description which could help locate the man, ripped directly from Jeannie Williams's own eyewitness testimony. It was issued to the press by Elphinstone Dalglish and remained, for a long time, one of the most granularly detailed descriptions of a murder suspect ever released to the Scottish media.

He is 25 to 30, 5ft 10in in height and of a medium build. Light auburn, reddish hair, brushed to the right. He has blue-grey eyes and nice straight teeth. But one tooth on the right overlaps the next. He has fine features and is generally of a smart, modern appearance. This man was known to have been dressed in a brownish flecked, single breasted suit with high lapels. His brownish coat – tweed or gaberdine – was worn knee length. His wrist-watch has a military-style strap (a thick strap with a thinner strap linked through it). He may smoke Embassy-tipped cigarettes and goes to the Barrowland Ballroom. He is thought to be called by his Christian name of John. He may speak of having a strict upbringing and make reference to the Bible. This man is quite well spoken, probably with a Glasgow accent, there may be marks on his face and hands.

***

It would be easy to push the idea that this marked the clearly defined start of the hysteria. The beginning of the fear and paranoia that was about to sweep across Glasgow in the following weeks and months following Helen Puttock's murder. And in a way, it was. Bible John was about to give a name and focus to the previously shapeless swell of violence that had been building in the city, though such changes seldom occur overnight, or perhaps hit quite so neatly as the usual accounts would have it. Even at the start of November 1969, there were other stories still jostling for attention. The violence just wouldn't stop, despite the christening of what the press were about to begin excitedly describing as the city's first truly modern serial killer. On 4 November, the papers had the story of a 17-year-old boy stabbed outside his home in Riddrie. He'd been attacked by a group of fellow teenagers and was said to be recovering at the Royal Infirmary, though there were no arrests to report. But one can trace the origins of the change in the coming days' papers. The way that the pace starts to pick up, with the story beginning to run slightly ahead of itself in the first flush of horrified enthusiasm.

Bible John had been born into a city that was only too ready to greet him.

THE BIRTH OF BIBLE JOHN

The first named appeal was all it took for the sightings to begin. By 5 November, police switchboards were inundated with calls. They were already arriving in their dozens, from all around the city and beyond. The head of the Marine Division CID out in Partick was keen to stress how seriously each tip-off was being treated. The contents of every call – he assured the press – were being checked out with painfully precise attention to detail, even if they were yet to find the man they were looking for.

For now, the focus was still fully trained on Helen Puttock, though police sources were publicly refusing to rule out a potential link between the two other Barrowland killings. Privately, there were those who were already advocating a longer, closer look at the similarities between the three murdered women. Though they might not say it out loud, it seemed to some detectives that an unignorable string of coincidences was beginning to link the crimes together. There was a growing conviction that a pattern was starting to emerge. A pattern, a hunch, a burst of hard-won professional intuition. Whatever they called it, it was soon to be very public knowledge.

Quietly at first, as on 6 November with a page 5 spread in the *Daily Record*. The piece carries a black-and-white photo the entire width of the page, trapped under the headline THE MEN WHO HUNT A KILLER. A soberly suited elderly man with drastically thinning hair stands at a heavy wooden desk, addressing his charges with the bearing of a reverend attending to his errant congregation. This is Elphinstone Dalglish holding a briefing for a room of over fifty detectives from around the city. Rows of jowly middle-aged men in heavy tweed suits and beige macs are captured listening intently to their superior. They had come to hear about Helen Puttock and Patricia Docker and Jemima MacDonald. About the figure now being called Bible John and the new weight of promising information offered up from the very first public appeal to use the new moniker. The camera catches a certain stuffy intensity, along with a few glazed faces caught by the flash.

One man is absent from the photograph. Joe Beattie was already a legendary figure in Glasgow, on both sides of the criminal divide. Born in the 1920s, he'd been raised on the Garscube Road, out in the West End. As a young

man, he'd had a respectably 'good war' serving as a
fighter pilot in Bomber Command, and had taken part in
several Allied raids across German territory. At the end of
hostilities, he had joined the then City of Glasgow Police
in 1946. Several histories have recorded his daring
exploits dating from his earliest years in the force. Anecdotes abound, particularly after his rapid promotion to
CID, which came in 1949. Physically, Beattie looked
exactly like what he was: a reassuringly solid star on the
rise. Tall, dark haired and possessing a legendarily intense
stare, he had made Detective Sergeant just a few years
after his arrival at CID. He had the gift – and that's how
it is always described, in half mystical terms – of often
simply finding himself in the right place at the right time.

His early exploits are often referred to in a strange,
airily imprecise tone; pitched somewhere between paper-
back crime caper and broad *Carry On* farce. There is the
incident with the barefoot man running through inner-
city Glasgow being chased by an increasingly breathless
Police Constable. When the zealous Beattie arrested the
man, it was revealed that his wife was about to give birth
and he and the officer running behind him had actually
been desperately searching for help. With no midwife
immediately available, Beattie and his beleaguered colleague helped deliver the baby themselves. Several
accounts like to highlight his carefully honed powers of

observation, developed from his years in the RAF (the causal link is apparently too obvious to require anything like a detailed explanation). Beattie was well known as a prolific murder solver, high or low profile, it didn't really matter. One particularly gory stabbing saw a breakthrough when he'd noticed a set of gleaming knives in a suspect's kitchen, so freshly cleaned that Beattie was certain they pointed to the man's guilt. Another case was helped along by the discovery of a Swan Vesta match found near the elderly victim's body. It's said that Beattie knew that men in the area never used that specific brand of match. Local door-to-door inquiries turned up a man who was asked to empty his pockets, which contained a Swan Vesta box.

These stories might strike the modern reader as little more than high journalistic camp, but every clipping contributed to the growing renown of Joe Beattie, indefatigable and incorruptible crime fighter. Something like a Glaswegian Sherlock Holmes, and a cosily authoritative buffer against the enveloping clouds of violence and despair looming over the city as the 1960s drew to a close.

In one heavily reported double-murder inquiry, Beattie was able to use his apparently superhuman powers of deduction to catch the killer of a man and his 17-year-old daughter who had been stabbed to death in their Kinning

Park home, a couple of miles south-west of the city centre. The killing had been random and frenzied, with each victim having been stabbed more than thirty times. The knife had been wiped of fingerprints and dumped in the kitchen, though Beattie was drawn to a toe print pressed on to the hallway linoleum (the killer had likely removed their socks and shoes so as not to catch any of the blood that coated the floor). During the following door-to-door inquiries, Beattie came across the 16-year-old neighbour who had rapidly emerged as the chief suspect. 'Not only did his toe print match the one found in the murder house', as one adoring profile puts it, 'but he also later confessed to the murder.' In 1968 alone, it's said that Beattie oversaw nine successful murder investigations.

By the turn of the decade, he had risen to Detective Superintendent. It wasn't all improbable, headline-grabbing murders. There was a clear-eyed shrewdness to Beattie. In Joe Jackson's *Chasing Killers*, he describes meeting Beattie for the first time as a young plain-clothes detective in the Northern Division, spending alternate night shifts with CID. Beattie was Detective Sergeant on the shift, partnered with another well-known face, a fellow DS called Tom MacDonald. They taught Jackson about interview techniques and how to cultivate inform-ants. Beattie in particular was well known for the sheer volume of eyes and ears he had on call in the West End, a

gallery of petty crooks and villains who grew to be affec-
tionately labelled 'Joe's half-crown touts'. He had an easy
way with superiors and underlings alike. Jackson writes
of Beattie and MacDonald how 'they were to the CID
what I [was] to the uniformed branch in that they were
forever locking up good criminals'. This well-cultivated
easy camaraderie had dissipated by November 1969. Joe
Jackson remembers bumping into his one-time mentor
not long after Beattie's promotion to Detective Chief
Inspector down at the Marine Division in Partick, a squat
stone block of pure Victorian Glasgow gothic. His for-
merly jovial superior, so well known for his perpetual
stream of wisecracks and indulgent advice, had shape-
shifted into a very different role. The new Beattie existed
at a deliberate remove from the men underneath him. He
took this role and his performance of it seriously. It was
'Mr Beattie' rather than 'Joe' by the time of Bible John's
first mention in the press, and had been so for quite some
time. Helen Puttock's body had been found in Mr Beattie's jurisdiction and it was, whatever anyone else might
think, Mr Beattie's responsibility to bring her killer to
justice.

Bible John kept cropping up in the tabloids across the
start of November. For now, it still mostly took the form
of neat little news items tucked into the inner pages.
There were other cruel, or desperately bizarre, stories that

required coverage. A delivery driver had found himself trapped in his refrigerated van and was only saved from an ignominious frozen death by an alert greengrocer, who wondered why the delivery was taking so long. This somehow made the front page of the *Daily Record* on 7 November, along with a considerably smaller piece devoted to Egypt's President Nasser declaring the inevitability of upcoming war with Israel. Bible John made it to page 7 the next day, with a brief little notice sharing an artist's impression of the killer's distinctive double-pocketed blazer. 'Do you recognise this jacket?' This was followed by the same public appeals for help, for any information that might lead detectives to the man said to be called John. The scripture-reciting figure with the reddish hair and crooked teeth. The sharp-featured, unusually well-mannered man suspected of killing Helen Puttock and perhaps the two other women taken from the Barrowland.

The details dripped down to the press from unnamed senior police sources. A new, more sophisticated photofit was put together – far outstripping the already quaint identikit sketch that had circulated in the press after Jemima MacDonald's murder – and instantly began to crop up on billboards and bus stops around the city. On the front page of the *Citizen* and the *Evening Times*. The new, stitched-together face staring back with inhuman blankness, despite its slightly curled lips wrapped into the first hint of a disdainful smile. THE REAL FACE OF BIBLE JOHN. This was not an identikit, the papers screamed. This was a photograph. Or rather, it was parts culled from many photographs, layered on top of one another to create a brand-new likeness. A brand-new face comprised of many others. The cutting-edge technique had been popularized by Jacques Penry, an English visual artist and successful former door-to-door Bible salesman with no scientific or academic background to speak of. Another first. Another confident step taken straight into the unknown. Have you seen this man? Did you know this man? The ghostly fugitive, already so desperately hunted by police across the city. Wanted: Bible John. Report all sightings to Glasgow Murder Inquiry Police. Tel. SEN 3500.

Even his most staunch defenders agreed that Joe Beattie was a man who thought in certainties. It's also often said that he was a man, a detective, rooted in the assumptions and prejudices of his time. To some, this is usually offered as an excuse for what came next, a pre-emptive *mea culpa* for the occasionally baroque weirdness that was to follow. Whatever the angle, almost every subsequent account agrees that there was no lip service paid to democracy down at Beattie's Marine Division. Mr Beattie wasn't a boss to be contradicted, or to be brought bad news. As the Helen Puttock murder inquiry picked up pace, the usual routine was at first adhered to. The working day was instantly transformed; eighteen-hour days became the norm, for the greenest detective right up to Joe Beattie and his avuncular second-in-command, George 'Yorkie' Lloyd. (His nickname, Joe Jackson writes in *Chasing Killers*, was due to his broad Yorkshire accent, 'almost making him a foreigner in those days'.) Beattie had his own finely styled personal procedural quirks. On visiting George Puttock in Earl Street the morning after his wife's murder, he'd asked him a simple question. Did he hit her? When he replied that he didn't, Beattie had asked him to strip. After closely inspecting Puttock's naked body for scratch marks, he'd explained that he was ever so sorry, but it couldn't be helped. In George Puttock's account, Beattie hadn't for a minute suspected the grieving husband, but it was just something he'd had to do.

From the very earliest days of the inquiry Joe Beattie had honed in on Jeannie Williams as his investigative ace card. The two were close right from the start, some have said almost inseparable at the peak of the investigation. Her very ordinariness and 'plain features' are often stressed. According to Samson and Crow, here was 'a typical hard-working Glesga' woman of the late 1960s'. Other clichés are employed to hammer this home. The diligent worker and mother, who didn't really want much else from life aside from a slightly bigger pay packet every week. Her new role was different. The murdered woman's sister and the only witness to her murderer. Joe Beattie had broken the news the day Helen Puttock's body had been discovered. Jeannie Williams had greeted the strange man at her front door with a smile, before he explained that her sister had been found by a dog walker in the back close on Earl Street.

The next weeks were a series of ever-more bitter struggles, but what else could they have been? The sisters had always been close. And there was no time to rest. No time for anything like grief or consideration of the facts of her sister's murder. The killing that was increasingly everywhere you might hope to turn in the city. On television and in newsprint, in papers half read and discarded on buses and subway carriages. The cause of horrified and excited chatter in pubs and office complexes from the West End right across to the Gallowgate, the apparently cursed epicentre of the murders. Joe Beattie was convinced that Jeannie Williams held the answers. Every single answer that might lead to the killer's identity. Everything in the detailed description now flooding the city came directly from her memories of the night her sister was killed. From the spectre's cruel thin facial features to the anachronistic cut of his suit. From the tone of his voice to his apparent propensity to lapse into scripture. Joe Beattie simply wasn't concerned with any other suspects or any other contradictory accounts. George Puttock was almost immediately discounted after his apparent run-in with Beattie and the fact of Jeannie's increasingly detailed testimony. None of the other potential witnesses were scouted. Castlemilk John hadn't come forward and couldn't be traced, while Beattie expressed little interest in speaking with the Barrowland manager who had handled the already fabled altercation at the cigarette machine.

Jeannie Williams had first visited the Marine Division the day after her sister's murder, where detectives had shown her a colourized copy of the identikit picture drawn after the Jemima MacDonald murder. During a later interview, she described a feeling akin to something turning in her guts. Like her intestines were churning with fear and recognition. The resemblance was there, she said. She'd shivered. The resemblance to what? To the man she had seen dancing with her sister under the lights at the Barrowland. To the tense, tightly coiled figure in the back of the taxi home. The pressure was there, squatting in the foreground, right from day one. The same lecturer, Lennox Paterson, was called back in from Glasgow School of Art to work on another depiction of the killer, urged on by Joe Beattie and Jeannie Williams's fresh testimony. The result is perhaps the most infamous visual contribution to the entire Bible John mythology. Though there are many similarities between the various official identikits and photofits, none quite has the same level of shockingly vivid detail or colour. The figure possesses neatly swept red hair and terrible, depthless bluish-grey eyes. You had to hand it to Paterson, Jeannie Williams said. That was the man she remembered (the man she had created under the glare of the Marine Division lights). The look on his face is one of tight, evangelical malice. Like the depiction of a devil in human form. This

Artist impression of Bible John

was not the usual kind of image employed in a serious murder investigation, and certainly not the sort of thing released to a fevered tabloid press desperate to make the most of the apparent serial killer prowling through the East End.

The publication of the new image wrenched something open in the public imagination. Though the newly detailed prose descriptions had provoked a respectable stream of information, no one was quite prepared for what came next. The introduction of the dead-eyed, red-haired spectre almost immediately blocked phone lines across the city's police divisions. There is a famous photo of a bemused detective unfurling a banner poster of a *Daily Record* front page emblazoned BARROWLAND MURDER: DO YOU KNOW BIBLE JOHN? It soon felt as if the entire city did – or wanted to believe so. Everyone seemed to recognize the figure, or knew someone who did. Detectives had gone to great lengths to make the newly disseminated image as accurate as possible. No expense or humiliation was spared. A dog had been chased down and sheared to capture a sample of hair that matched Jeannie Williams's vision to the most minute shade of auburn. People had begun to see Bible John everywhere. In pubs, on trains and sloping down suburban high streets. The phone lines jammed and the case files fattened. Jeannie Williams would be called away from her work at McLarens Controls on West Street to eyeball the latest array of men pulled in from every corner of the city.

The calls weren't confined to Glasgow. They arrived from right across the country, down to the furthest reaches of southern England and far beyond. Every sighting was checked out by a weary detective trudging up a suburban driveway armed with a picture of the uncaught killer, or braving the stairs of a high-rise block to listen patiently to the latest theory or accusation. People were scared, a fear that often bled into excitement. Bible John could mean opportunity. How better to flatten an ancient grudge, or settle a long-simmering dispute? Neighbours fell under suspicion. Husbands and uncles, brothers and sons. Few of the young or almost young were really above scrutiny. Tolerance wasn't part of the new mood. The picture's ambiguity was part of it. There were a lot of Johns in Glasgow and even more men with red hair. In an early 1970s TV interview, one man recalls being hauled in front of Beattie at the Marine Division HQ. It's true, the similarities to the artist's impression are undeniable. With his red hair and angular face, it could be a seaside sketch of the young man, an easy 25–30, sitting in his living room. He hadn't just been picked up once, he explains with a laugh. And each time Beattie had complimented him on a rare likeness to the killer. Beattie was always friendly, the man explains. He couldn't stop calling him son. Did that cheer you up, the unseen interviewer asks. The question contorts the man's face. No, he might be able to speak about it now, but he can't deny he was worked up at the time.

Not everyone placed the same blind faith in Jeannie Williams's testimony as Joe Beattie. It had been late, she'd had a drink. And her sister had been murdered. Strangled and discarded in an alleyway a few yards from her home. Of course she wanted to be useful in the hunt for the killer, though some privately wondered at the pressure being exerted on her. There was a constant stream of line-ups and identity parades. Jeannie Williams attended them all, but none of the faces was the right face. There were hundreds of men put forward in those early weeks, a blur of red-haired young men, always different, always the same. Frustration began to line the face of detectives. But Joe Beattie didn't waver. He had his witness and his own clearly defined suspect that resided in his mind, and his mind alone. Though even Beattie wasn't above proffering some slight tweaks. They began to attempt a new tactic, whereby Jeannie Williams was asked to grade suspects out of a hundred against their physical likeness to the man she had been in the taxi with. Some were to come up in the high nineties.

By December, it was clear that this first manic flush of activity was no closer to locating the uncaught killer. The world outside the Marine incident room hadn't stopped.

There were still other murders to attend to, other killings that jostled hard for space with Bible John. Charles Manson was starting to become a fixture of the international pages (*HIPPIE MURDER CULT PLANNED 11 MORE DEATHS*), while more locally, a 20-year-old from Possil was found guilty of beating a police officer to death (a tranche of conservative law-and-order editorials followed, bemoaning a succession of spineless, overly liberal Home Secretaries who were accused of fostering a culture of impunity, of disregard for the forces of authority). Horror on every page you turned. The 12 December edition of the *Daily Record* carried a front page detailing the story of a Lanarkshire man who had just been jailed for life for murdering his ex-wife in a jealous rage. He had beaten her, before strangling her with her own tights. Arnot McWhinnie reported how the family wept as the verdict was announced at the High Court in Glasgow. An elderly woman had gone missing and was presumed dead, possibly killed. Ian Brady made the paper a few days later, having been involved in a vicious prison fight (*MOORS MAN BRADY IN FIGHT WITH CHILD KILLER*). The next day's front page focused on an Edinburgh man who had been convicted after torturing his two young children. Mention of Bible John is only tucked into the inner pages of that day's paper. Viewers of a late-night religious programme on STV had anxiously phoned in to the Marine after seeing a man in the audience who they were sure was the killer. Joe Beattie is quoted, reassuring the public that this was not the man they were searching for. Detectives had combed through the footage, and Beattie was satisfied that '[while] the facial characteristics were similar [the] hairstyle was not'. Instead, he took the time to renew his already proffered appeal. Someone out there had to know Bible John. 'The man we want to interview could be anybody. Your next-door neighbour or your friend. It is absolutely vital that we trace him.'

The young Joe Jackson was called in during early January 1970, after the decision had been taken to freshen up an investigation that had seen detectives putting in at least fourteen-hour days without a break for the entirety of the previous three months. By then there was the beginning of the sense, Jackson writes, that things had started to grow stale. None of the identity parades had yet turned up a decent suspect, or even a significant witness. On 30 December, a police officer had been shot dead by a group of armed robbers at 51 Allison Street in Govanhill, after an attempted arrest that had rapidly gone wrong. In the aftermath, resources and column inches found themselves directed to the Southside, at least for a short while. But Bible John was still in vogue. The Barrowland trade had yet to pick up and its managers were anxious, as the idea of a serial killer stalking the dancehall wasn't proving good for consumer confidence.

Joe Jackson and the group of new detectives were given strict directions regarding the man they were seeking. One of the new lines of inquiry involved visiting dentists across Glasgow and Strathclyde. Jeannie Williams had apparently told Beattie that the man in the taxi had a slight deformity in his front teeth, with the right crossing slightly over the left. It was also said that the man would be missing his fourth upper-right tooth, a level of detail that some detectives thought implausibly precise. How, they wondered privately, would it have been possible to see it in the back of a dimly lit taxi? The dentists Joe Jackson spoke with expressed the same misgivings. Though the slight overlap could be noticeable, the missing tooth would likely only be discernible through a full dental examination. None of this deterred Joe Beattie, who commissioned experts at Glasgow Dental School to make a plaster cast that mirrored the spectral killer's much-theorized-over mouth (Helen Puttock's body had been riven by several deep bite marks). When TV reporters asked a visibly exhausted and gaunt-faced Beattie why he kept it in his desk drawer, his answer came wrapped in a tight, slightly embarrassed smile. Despite it being dutifully photographed and disseminated to every dentist's surgery on the West Coast of Scotland, nothing of any use rebounded back. In those first months, 920 doctors and dentists were interviewed by a revolving cast of increasingly beleaguered detectives, searching for something, anything, to dignify the plaster cast lying untouched in their boss's desk drawer. Was it true, as one reporter asked Beattie, that they were rapidly approaching the dry and desperate stage? The response was both firm and acidic. 'No, we're anything but dry and desperate. [We have] half a dozen good tricks up our sleeve that we can and will use, if we don't get the phone call or the information we're seeking. But we're far, far from being dry and desperate.'

One of these tricks involved the formation of what the press were to delightedly call the 'Marine Formation Dancing Team' (some simply went with the 'Bible John Dancing Squad'). The premise was simple enough. Teams of plain-clothes detectives were dispatched to the city's dancehalls three times a week, from the Barrowland to the Majestic and the Plaza. The brief was to dance with the clientele while quizzing them about their movements and whether they'd encountered any scripture-obsessed men named John in the course of their evenings out. Results were predictably thin, particularly on Thursday nights at the Barrowland where the straight-laced plain-clothes detectives collided with the implicit culture of silence and secrecy. Over 240 tailors were questioned to establish whether any of them might have sold a distinctive 'continental-style suit' to a man fitting Bible John's description. Golf courses across Scotland saw detectives swarm their clubhouses, looking for lists of anyone that had recently shot a hole in one. The specially constructed incident room at the Marine Division had become a barely functional mass of papers and witness statements. Jeannie Williams remained a fixture at the station, poring through photos and case files with Joe Beattie in the smoke-filled office, right through until the early hours. Meanwhile, the sightings kept on coming. Men picked up from street corners on an anonymous tip-off, or at the whims of overstretched and overzealous police patrols. Churches were monitored, with little success. The paranoia drifted beyond the city. One spooked Edinburgh taxi driver drove straight to the nearest police station after his fare had innocently made reference to the Bible in the course of their polite chit-chat.

Joe Beattie and his team continued to funnel information to their trusted reporters at the same interconnected web of tabloids, who greedily scooped up any new details on the terrible killer, still thought to be roaming the streets uncaught. Sales boomed. A specially chosen police officer was given the full-time job of sending the photofit to every police station across Britain. Beattie began to fixate on the idea that the man might have been in the armed forces, due to the time separating the killings and the apparent fact – so threadbare and tightly held to – of the killer's short hair. Detectives visited barracks and army camps, RAF airfields and naval bases. Nothing came back. The crews of ships berthed in the Clyde at the time of Helen Puttock's murder were inspected and immediately released. It was decided that the killer might have a mental disorder that explained his actions. Every hospital in Glasgow was visited and every patient list pored over. And still nothing came back. Three deserters from the armed forces were court-martialled after an intense round of questioning. Over 5,000 men were questioned in the first year of the inquiry alone. Police began to issue cards to the most unfortunate men who had been picked up repeatedly. It carried the direct number for George Lloyd and would serve as grounds for instant release.

There was a strangeness beginning to cloud the air down at the Marine and almost everyone could feel it seeping into the most mundane day-to-day procedure. Joe Jackson and a colleague were asked to pick up a man from Lennoxtown, a small town out in the East Dunbartonshire boondocks. He'd phoned in to say that he'd had a vision that told him Bible John was living in a flat above a chip shop, along with a woman who had a young child. Jackson was ordered to pick the man up and deposit him at the office where he was to be interviewed by Joe Beattie, with Jeannie Williams in attendance. The meeting did not go well and ended, according to Jackson, with the medium hurtling through the front door without his feet touching the ground. He was later deposited back in East Dunbartonshire after a cup of tea and some soothing words.

It was not the inquiry's best-known brush with the supernatural. In March 1970, the internationally renowned Dutch clairvoyant Gerard Croiset had flown into Glasgow from his home in Utrecht to much press fanfare, after reading about the hunt for the freshly christened serial killer in the international media. In a sign of the growing desperation, Beattie welcomed the strange figure into the Marine and had him draw up a crude 'profile'. He asked for minimal details and was given them. Croiset then picked up a pen and began to draw, to the barely suppressed scepticism of assembled detectives. He sketched out a map of the city and scrawled over the area where the killer would likely be found. In his vision, Bible John was no older than 28 and a young man who almost certainly counted body-building among his interests, despite the slim figure staring out from the various composite images that had flooded the city. The killer was tall and walked erect with his shoulders back and chest puffed out. Officers were immediately dispatched to search the area of the Southside that Croiset had marked on his paper. They visited shops and schools, factories and parks, and nothing – nothing at all – came back with them. The infamous psychic was to leave for home after forty-eight hours. Joe Beattie's reaction to his departure is not recorded.

George Puttock had agreed to take part in a press conference. It was reported that this represented another first, for the husband of a murdered woman to appeal in public for any information relating to her murder. He spoke to the crush of assembled reporters from the back of a grey, cramped Glasgow courtroom. Most subsequent accounts approve of his performance and praise his dramatic intervention.

I'd like to ask this man John to consider me and my two children. This thing has ruined my career. I am a corporal in the Royal Signals, awaiting promotion. I have done 11 years and now I will have to leave. And I've been left with my two children, five-year-old David and baby Michael. Their mother loved the children. So do I and I can't bear to be a weekend father now they have lost their mother. I hope this appeal will help bring this man to justice. Everything else has failed so far. The police have worked their guts out, but no-one has so far supplied the clue that will help trap this monster.

A £200 reward was later posted using George Puttock's own money. Plain-clothes CID had attended Helen Puttock's funeral at Lambhill Cemetery on the northern fringes of the city, mixing with mourners in the hope that the killer wouldn't be able to resist showing up. But the burial passed quietly, without incident or any sinister visitations.

Whatever Joe Beattie's public proclamations, it was clear that a raggedness had set into the constantly sprawling investigation operating out of the Marine. You could see it by looking at a man who never seemed to sleep or consider anything else other than Bible John. His increasingly erratic decision-making and heavy reliance on Jeannie Williams were beginning to cause alarm, though not yet enough to see Beattie directly challenged. He began to repeat that he would know the killer by sight, as if it were simply a matter of divine inspiration. This was Mr Beattie's case. The kind of hunt that might transfigure a respected detective into something more, something perhaps akin to a living legend.

There is a famous image of Beattie taken a few years later, of the once ubiquitous DSI posing outside the

Police chief Joe Beattie

Barrowland, some time after the very pinnacle of his power and authority and the peak of the initial investigation into what were almost universally now being referred to as the Bible John murders. He stands alone at the forefront of the frame, his piercing dark eyes peering somewhere beyond the camera, past the rain-slicked Gallowgate, with a mostly unlit Barrowland looming to his right. The greasy concrete is partially cut through by the reflection of the streetlights in the background. But the streets are devoid of any life, save for the tweed-suited protector staring wide-eyed out into the night.

* * *

I arrived at 226 Gallowgate on a sad night towards the end of summer 2022. It had been raining hard and I'd been soaked through on my walk from the Mitchell Library. The sun was out and then it wasn't, with the change occurring before anyone really knew what to do about it. In town, I'd walked past a procession of brollies hurriedly opening in a disjointed, fretful performance. I suppose my daydreams must have been especially diverting, because I didn't seem to notice the sky until much later than everyone else, until it was too late to protect myself.

The afternoon had passed with everything I could find about Joe Beattie. His words in the press and on film, as well as the accounts of his contemporaries, admiring and otherwise. I'd been thinking about how every classic crime legend needs its avenging angel somewhere in the mix. Its incorruptible force for good to set against the crush of darkness. The misery and pain. And how reality can never really quite conform to these storybook conventions. I thought about these things, and what I'd read detailing the overheated and painfully myopic investigation that began after the murder of Helen Puttock. About Joe Beattie's ever-escalating obsession with the killer the press had dubbed Bible John.

I continued to think about what it meant to have said, as Beattie famously once did, that he knew more about this richly constructed figure than he did about members of his own family. That he'd know him instantly if he walked into even the most crowded of rooms.

The bar has a faintly sad feeling clinging to it when I arrive, with its rows of neat and non-threateningly trendy furniture entirely empty save for the friend I'm meeting, who lives close by and whose grandmother had lived on the Gallowgate for most of her life until she died a few years back. Do you remember, he asks me, how this spot used to be the Bairds Bar, the wild old Celtic pub that was shuttered after one too many bloody bar fights and deliberate provocation to the licensing board? And I think I do vaguely, or maybe I'd just read about it or caught some ribald anecdotes second hand somewhere. Not that it really matters. We order drinks and talk a bit about our days, until I make my excuses and head outside for a cigarette now that the rain has retreated as quickly as it had attacked. The Barrowland sits next door, as faded and solid and majestic as ever. There're a few weak beams of sun fighting their way out of the horizon to the west, though I reckon the streets could well be just as wet and empty as they were in the black-and-white photo of Joe Beattie taken over half a century ago.

HE KNEW HIS BIBLE,
HE WAS VERY CLEVER

There was only to be disappointment for those wishing that the new decade would bring any greater clarity to the inquiry. In September 1970, the telephone switchboard at the Marine had jammed again after a BBC *Current Account* programme had aired, which ended with a personal appeal from presenter, Hugh Cochrane. The tone is mollifying and almost wearily paternalistic, with the killer urged to hand himself in. 'If you are out there watching, maybe it is time for you to come out of the glare for your own good.' Over 350 calls arrived at the Marine almost as soon as the message had broadcast at 9 p.m. The same deluge, yet again. The same excited rush of names and dates, and sinister faces glimpsed for a moment at night through rain-streaked bus windows, or smirking at the bar in this or that godforsaken pub on a packed Saturday night.

Joe Beattie was still determined to offer a showcase from his self-described box of tricks, however thin the performance was beginning to feel as the days went on. There was to be some more added novelty. A Glaswegian psychiatrist, Dr Robert Brittain, was hired to produce a criminal profile of the imagined suspect (it is often explained in reports that stress Beattie's brilliance that this predated the much-mythologized efforts of the FBI by several years). The result was full of further headline-grabbing details. Bible John was a sadistic murderer. He was likely a loner (and had been so throughout his life) and would have begun his deviant behaviour in child-hood. Brittain was also certain that the killer had strangled his victims to prolong his own sexual pleasure, despite the lack of solid evidence.

The strain was beginning to tell. The long days and endless nights, chasing the latest threadbare leads and accusations. Several accounts highlight the string of broken police marriages that began to accumulate in the first year of what was now simply being referred to as the Bible John inquiry (the name had already been proven to sell far more papers than Docker or MacDonald or Puttock could by themselves). Days and nights would pass at the Marine, and still nothing tangible. No killer, no suspect and no one else's word in the matter other than that of Joe Beattie. Of all the subsequent memoirs of the era's self-avowedly hard-bitten detectives, few are as scathing towards Beatie as that of Les Brown, a former Detective Superintendent (his 2005 *Glasgow Crimefighter* is billed as the true story of one of Glasgow's most controversial detectives and his battle with the criminals and violent street gangs of the city). Naturally, the pugnacious detective had thought it prudent to wait forty years before spilling the explosive details of his dissatisfaction.

In Brown's extraordinary telling, he outlines a lead he'd pursued in the summer of 1970. There was a man using the pseudonym 'John White' living on St Andrews Street, in the city centre. When this turned out to be a false address, Brown had tried to bring him into the Marine. The man seemed to fit the Bible John mould, in almost every conceivable way, right down to his hair and attire. But Beattie had rejected him out of hand, for reasons that Brown could never quite fathom. This story is, one supposes, an attempt to highlight a wider truth about Beattie's almost imperial arrogance and inflexibility. Though its author didn't come out particularly well from it, post publication. 'John White' read Brown's account in the papers after the book received modest press attention and instantly offered to provide a DNA sample to categorically rule himself out of any further connection to the sorry ongoing saga.

The weeks passed and the phone calls and sightings began to dry up, though few wanted to admit publicly or privately that this was the case. By the end of 1970, the spectre of Bible John had begun a slow drift from the inner pages of the *Daily Record* and *Evening Times*, while the broadsheets had long diverted their attention elsewhere from the tawdry reams of speculation that flowed from the Barrowland murders. Still, milestones were reached. It was admiringly said that the Puttock manhunt alone was already the largest in Scottish legal history and perhaps the most expensive, though few accurate figures supporting that have ever been released. Jeannie Williams slowly became less and less of a feature down at the Marine and the whispers about the depth of her involvement in the inquiry began to gradually abate. She returned, for a time, to everyday obscurity, left to mourn her sister alone, away from the glare of the press. The three murders and their ghostly uncaught killer began to recede from the foreground. You didn't have to look far for other horrors, in Glasgow or beyond, and even Joe Beattie was forced to divert his gaze as the heat began to drain from the Helen Puttock investigation.

Sixty-six football fans were crushed to death at Ibrox Stadium on 2 January 1971 at the end of the traditional New Year 'Old Firm' derby between Rangers and Celtic. Beattie had attended the game and had made his way home afterwards, entirely unaware of the desperate scenes that had seen a further 200 people badly injured, as well as the dozens killed. The phone call had arrived right from the very top, from the then Chief Constable, Sir James Robertson, who had told Beattie in no uncertain terms that he was to take charge of the inquiry. The subsequent investigation was run from Govan Police Office, where over a thousand statements were collected from fans and other eyewitnesses, including police officers and the emergency service people who had attended the scene. 'Such was the swiftness and efficiency of his investigation', as one subsequent account puts it, 'that a Fatal Accident Inquiry was held into the deaths the following month at Pollokshaws Burgh Hall in Glasgow.' It is spelled out that this was Joe Beattie at his methodical best; a very different figure, almost unrecognizable, from the brooding obsessive who had attached himself so closely to Bible John.

Other fragments crop up from the time that appear to show another, almost mystically perceptive Beattie. One morning during the Ibrox Disaster investigation, he was contacted and told to make his way to Glasgow Sheriff Court, to supervise a dispute between a Cypriot restaurant owner named Nicholas Perdikou and his legion of creditors. An informant had passed on gossip that the desperate Perdikou was likely armed and had hatched a plan to shoot the sheriff who was in the process of hearing the case. Beattie caught Perdikou on a stairwell at the court and frisked open his coat to reveal a shotgun and cartridge belt. The beleaguered restaurateur was sent down for nine months and had his gun licence revoked.

By the late winter of 1971, it was increasingly impossible to ignore the drift in public or press attention. Bible John was becoming stale and police bosses were growing nervous at the lack of results, despite the expense and sheer unrelenting volume of time and effort that had already been unquestioningly pumped into the inquiry. A decision was taken to row back and think again. Beattie's fiefdom down in Partick had to be addressed and, after the successful Ibrox Disaster investigation, he was moved to the Scottish Police Training College at Tulliallan Castle in Fife, where he was made Deputy Commandant before taking retirement in 1976, barely into his midfifties. It's hard to say whether the move was intended as subtle punishment or reward. His reaction to shifting cross country is not recorded, though the Bible John inquiry rapidly begins to recede from the press after this time, bar the odd excited notice in one or another of Glasgow's tabloids. It was later recalled how often Beattie would speak on Bible John to recruits under his tutelage. If a lecturer failed to show up, then Beattie would have no problem picking up the slack, picking up the opportunity to speak on his favourite subject. It seemed to colleagues as if the case was never too far from the surface. As if the old obsession was as potent as it had ever been.

Life in the city continued as the new decade opened out. In 1975, the storied old City of Glasgow Police found itself merged with several surrounding forces to become Strathclyde Police. Fashions changed and the unsolved killings continued to accumulate. For the most opportunistic in the press or elsewhere, there was always a link to be made with Bible John, particularly if the murdered woman had last been seen at an entertainment venue or her handbag hadn't been recovered. If nothing else, it could prove a reliable momentary publicity boost, even if the link didn't quite take hold in the public imagination. In August 1977, a 20-year-old brewery worker called Anna Kenny had got chatting to two men in a city-centre-pub smoking area during a night out with friends. At closing time, she had left with one of the men and they'd made their way to George Square, where she caught a bus home to the Gorbals. She was later seen walking in Townhead, where she probably hailed a taxi before vanishing into the night. Her body was found twenty months later in rural Argyll, over 100 miles from home. Two shepherds had come across her grave on a remote corner of land under a hillside. Her neck and ankles had been bound. In October 1977, a 36-year-old woman named

Hilda McAuley had visited the Plaza Ballroom in the Southside, after leaving her two young boys with her mother. Not much detail is ever given about her life, though reports at the time invariably mention her divorce eight years previously. Her body was discovered the next day by a group of children, who were playing in some woods out in Langbank, Renfrewshire. She had suffered severe head injuries before her body had been discarded in a patch of long grass. Her coat, shoes and handbag were missing and never recovered.

In December 1977, a 23-year-old nurse named Agnes Cooney had spent the evening at the Clada Club on Westmoreland Street, a few hundred yards from the Plaza. Around 200 people attended the same country-and-western gig and Cooney had left the venue in the early hours, after the promise of a lift home. Her body was discovered by a farmer the next morning, on a quiet stretch of road in Lanarkshire. She had been stabbed twenty-four times. In 1978, the body of a 17-year-old girl named Mary Gallacher was discovered near Springburn train station. She had been beaten to death and likely sexually assaulted.

The years passed, marked by fresh killings and violence. For many, the Bible John murders had simply become a historical curio by the dawn of the 1980s. They already seemed like a distant series of occurrences; the dancehalls, the formal clothing, the images of the murdered women staring back from black-and-white photographs. There are no publicly available records to show how many sightings continued to drip into police records, if any did at all. The city still held the same problems as well as joys. Half-demolished buildings were still a regular sight, too regular to really be remarked upon. In 1980, a young and already distinguished French photographer called Raymond Depardon was commissioned by the *Sunday Times* magazine to photograph Glasgow. Depardon, who had never been to the city and could only speak a few words of English, immediately trained his lens on the city's slums and fading docklands. The result was a brilliant, often moving collection, even if its focus was entirely trained on the Glasgow that would appeal most to shocked and titillated readers elsewhere. A world of wide-open and empty industrial landscapes, contrasted with soot-blackened rows of tenements and images of solitary young mothers pushing their prams across gritted paths, backdropped by looming grey high-rise flats.

But Bible John was too stubborn to disappear entirely. In early February 1983, a strange development came to temporarily dominate the front pages of Glasgow's tabloids. *IS THIS THE FACE OF BIBLE JOHN?* asked the front page of the *Daily Record*, next to a spread on the untimely death of international 'pop sensation' Karen Carpenter. A new image had helpfully been drawn up for the morning paper, of a scowling thin-faced figure with a shadow cast over him (the incredible news came a day after the same paper had published a straight-faced denunciation of the cheque-book journalism that had just been eviscerated in the two-year inquiry that had followed the trial of 'the Yorkshire Ripper', Peter Sutcliffe).

> *For almost two years a Bible-quoting fiend brought terror to the dance-halls of Glasgow. His victims ... three innocent young mothers he strangled after nights out in the city's Barrowland Ballroom ... Now detectives are back on the 15-year-old trail of the notorious killer ... thanks to dramatic new evidence handed to the police by the Daily Record. And the full-scale hunt is on again for a man of evil.*

The information had come from a man initially identified only as Harry X, a Glasgow businessman who had made contact with two of the city's best-known private detectives, Bill Blyth and Richard McCue (the accompanying pictures show two seemingly mild-mannered men with an uncanny resemblance to Peter Cook and Dudley Moore). The duo had an unusually well-developed reputation for scrupulousness and had initially been unsure about the slightly fevered phone call that had come through to their offices from a man claiming to know Bible John's identity.

It was an old schoolfriend, the man had explained. His suspicion had been piqued when he'd come across a late 1970s news article on the killer that listed the familiar details, illustrated by the famous artist's impression. With his having lived abroad during the height of the initial frenzy, the story had mostly passed Harry X by. But after five years of agonizing doubt, he was sure of what he had to do. There was no way he was mistaken. The more he spoke, the more the two detectives were intrigued, and they eventually took on the case with one proviso, that they would keep any mention of it under wraps until they were sure there was at least a reasonable chance that the stream of accusations might be true. It is somewhat surprising, then, to consider that they enlisted the *Daily Record* to help compile 'the dossier on the murder mystery'. The files contained photos and drawings, dates and addresses, work history and social habits, as well as a rudimentary psychological profile.

Though the detectives admit they initially felt ridiculous, nothing had arrived to seriously dissuade them. They had, the report mentions, tracked down Jeannie Williams and showed her photographs of six different young men, and she had pointed out the figure from the dossier. They were able to establish that 'Harry's friend' had been in Glasgow at the time of the murders, though he had been living away from the city in the years since.

They had also found out where he was living now. Harry X and the unnamed 'suspect' had been close in their early twenties, young working-class men who, like so many others, spent their leisure time at the dancing in the 1960s. Harry X explained how they'd end up at the Barrowland on a Thursday night, mostly downstairs at Geordie's Byre. They were often, unapologetically, out on the pull, though this particular friend had a thing for the married women upstairs. He was tall and slim, with unfashionably short brown hair and invariably immaculate clothes. Though hailing from an unprepossessing part of the East End, 'he knew his Bible' and was 'very clever and articulate' at school. The piece also alludes to 'certain aspects of his home life' that might have made him develop a particularly strong dislike of married women socializing on their own, despite his own apparent sexual tastes. Though his accuser knew it sounded ridiculous, he couldn't bear living with the strain and guilt any longer.

The papers strung it out for all it was worth, with front pages on the *Evening Times* and a week-long series of features and reactive pieces in the *Daily Record*. Strathclyde Police had taken the dossier seriously, at least in public, with the latest CID boss, Detective Chief Superintendent John McDougall, wheeled out to speak to reporters of the formal ongoing investigation into the new developments. Joe Beattie was tracked down at his home in Bearsden to give his say on the matter. Though long retired he had never given up, he explains, and had been happy to assist the two PIs in their inquiry, even to the point of sharing his personal Bible John files. It had lived with him, he says. Nothing had been diluted. He was as anxious today as when he was first handed the case, fifteen years before. He'd still know the guy when he came eye to eye with him. He should have got him and remained convinced that he'd merely been unlucky. He'd used every move available to him, and then some more. Though he was sure they knew everything about the killer, he concedes that they never really got a sniff at him. Beattie passed on his regards to John McDougall and wished him the good fortune he was sure he'd been denied.

Harry X turned out to be Harry Wylie, a 36-year-old businessman who had spent years living in Australia before returning to Glasgow in the late 1970s. On 10 February, the *Daily Record* beamed out another self-proclaimed 'Great Exclusive'. *I'M NOT BIBLE JOHN* contained the first words from the mysterious suspect referred to in the new dossier, a Glaswegian ex-pat named David Henderson. It was outrageous, he said from his home in Holland, which he shared with his Austrian wife and two young children. It has to be remarked that the resemblance to the artist's impression is uncanny. Henderson scowls out from the

page as a youthful 36, with angular cheekbones and quizzical, almost suspicious eyes (it is unrealistic perhaps to
expect a man accused of serial murder to be smiling too
broadly). Yes, he was aware of the likeness and yes, he'd
attended the Barrowland in his twenties, though that was
as far as any of it went. He was quite willing to be interviewed by the police, though had decided against coming
back to Scotland to clear his name for the time being, if
only to avoid the inevitable media scrum. He told the *Daily
Record* reporters who had turned up at his door that there
was no way of saying exactly what he'd been doing at the
time of the killings. He might have been in Glasgow, or he
might have been away. He'd travelled all over, right from
his earliest twenties. London, the Midlands, the Channel
Islands, Germany and Holland. When news of the accusation had been broken, he'd greeted it with incredulous
laughter, even if he 'wouldn't wish this kind of suspicion on
his worst enemy'.

His first thought was that he had no idea what his old
friend was trying to achieve with the dossier. And even if
he was to admit to a slight likeness, he didn't have
crooked teeth or auburn hair. As for the Barrowland: it
was just where everyone went, but he was adamant that
it had never really been his sort of place. Anyway, it was
Harry Wylie who was always getting into fights and had
to be bailed out by his understanding, if perpetually

exasperated friends. The two had lost touch in their late twenties, though he added the tender little detail that they'd almost 'been like brothers' in their earlier years. Henderson explains to the reporters that he has a week to prepare for major surgery to treat an unnamed sleeping sickness, and that this surreal episode couldn't have come at a worse time. His wife is quoted in the piece, saying that it would be impossible to live with a man for twelve years 'and not know every bit of his soul'. She had met Harry Wylie once in London, though she would like to see him again, if only to give him a piece of her mind.

The publicity was to blow back so badly that Harry Wylie (there is a tiny picture scraped into the bottom of the page that shows a heavy-set, bearded man with a look of purely wounded bafflement spread across his face) was forced to go into temporary hiding, away from his family in Lanarkshire and his thriving heating business in Dennistoun. Henderson was quizzed by detectives and swiftly ruled out before the story sank without a trace, save for one brief piece, again in the *Daily Record*. MANHUNT FOR A FIEND ALWAYS ENDED IN FAILURE, by Gordon Airs, details the run of apparent 'prime suspects' that had slipped through the net without a single arrest, despite the police interviews that had taken place across the UK and beyond, from Germany to Zambia and Hong Kong. It speculates that Bible John would probably be living a normal life by now, just like David Henderson, the unfortunate Glaswegian family man abroad, caught up and discarded in a surreal web of accusation and intrigue. There are some comforting words from 'a leading psychiatrist' called Dr Hunter Gillies, who remained certain that the mysterious figure would have simply grown out of his 'psychopathic tendencies' so many years on from the dreadful murders of Patricia Docker, Jemima MacDonald and Helen Puttock.

David Henderson and Harry Wylie returned to permanent obscurity soon after this piece. One would like to know if they ever met or corresponded again, or if that was the end of Wylie's suspicions and he simply returned to fretting about business rates and the latest developments in the heating industry. The *Daily Record* moved on swiftly enough. As ever, there were fresher killings to contend with, which were to knock the old Bible John saga from top billing. Just a day after David Henderson's dramatic interview came a new and even bolder front page. The remains of seventeen young men had been discovered at two properties across North London, at 23 Cranley Gardens in Muswell Hill and another house three miles away on Melrose Avenue, Willesden Green. The next day's papers announced that a Scottish man named Dennis Andrew Nilsen had been arrested and charged with their murders.

THE REPORTER I

The more time I spent at the *Daily Record* archives, the more impossible it became to ignore Arnot McWhinnie. The paper's ex-chief crime reporter was everywhere I turned, from the late-1960s to the mid-1990s. Whenever a major crime story flashed up, so would the McWhinnie byline. A dizzying, decades-spanning blur of murders and robberies, rapes and shootings. He had been on Bible John from the very start, having joined the *Daily Record* in 1967 after a brief stint as a court reporter at a rival Glasgow paper, just a year before Patricia Docker's killing.

It took a while to get in touch with the veteran former crime reporter. He had left the paper in 1994 to set up a press agency covering Scotland's courts, along with a couple of former colleagues. The *Glasgow Herald* had bemoaned the ending of an era, with the giants of the golden age bowing out to usher in a new, far less self-confident and agenda-setting paper. McWhinnie finally retired in 2008 with a 100-person congregation from Glasgow's media and legal professions turning out to pay tribute to 'one of the great names in Scottish journalism', as he is described in a piece detailing the event held in the precincts of Glasgow's High Court.

It was time, the same article explains, for McWhinnie to attend to his passions for angling and shooting near his Perthshire home. In the autumn of 2022, I'd tracked down the home phone number of the once ubiquitous former crime reporter from a mutual work acquaintance. At first, McWhinnie sounded reticent. He was beginning to write his memoirs and didn't want to rehash too much of what he was planning to document, though he soon softened when I explained precisely what it was I wanted to know. Such as what the newsroom had felt like during that first flush of Bible John hysteria in 1969, and whether he had any qualms – then or now – about the evident closeness between police and press.

Our conversation has been edited for length and clarity.

Arnot McWhinnie: I'd been a court reporter at an evening paper before moving to the *Daily Record* as Chief Crime Reporter. That's when I started and I was there for another twenty-seven years. [After that] I formed a freelance agency called the Glasgow Court Agency, which covered all the High Court and Sheriff Court trials.

I've covered just about everything over that time, practically every major Scottish crime and court story.

Francisco Garcia: Even when you go back to the late 1960s, there's this narrative that has developed where it was Bible John and nothing else. When in reality, the papers were dominated by all sorts of killings and violent crime.

AM: Crime, next to sport, was the biggest seller of papers in that era. We had gang crime and whatever else. In those days, a murder was a murder and the papers were deeply interested, even if it was just two young gangsters that had been in a fight, with one lying dead. The papers wanted to know absolutely everything about the deceased, his background and all the rest of it.

Then there'd be the background on the killer, with photos and more detail. It was treated in a big way. A murder was a murder and it was usually front page. These days, a murder is nothing. It might not even get printed in the papers, or it's just three or four paragraphs.

FG: It's striking to see the difference, the level of detail between then and the present day. It's almost a different form. As if it's hardly the same thing at all.

AM: No. I mean, news editors wanted to know every spit and fart to be honest with you. It's not the same nowadays. It used to be that reporters physically fought to get their stories. I mean there were punch-ups and all the rest of it. If someone got off with a crime, was not guilty or whatever else, and a rival paper bought him up and whisked him away, well it would be big, big news.

FG: What was the *Record* like at the time? It was the main game in town then, right?
AM: It was. Well, it wasn't when I'd joined. The biggest-selling paper was the *Scottish Daily Express*, which was a broadsheet. They had a huge staff. Whenever you'd be out on a job, you'd be outmuscled by three of their reporters and photographers. You had to work doubly hard to get your story.

The political situation changed over the years in Scotland. The *Express* was a Tory newspaper and much of Scotland was Conservative voting. Labour gradually began to take over and the *Record* was a Labour-supporting paper. The readership went up and up and up until, quite frankly, we did the *Express* in and they folded in Scotland. There were great celebrations when our circulation went above theirs. It was a great victory. We used to sell 780,000 copies each and every day.

Virtually everyone in Scotland read the *Record*. It was a tabloid of course, and it continued to become an ever-better tabloid. We were probably the most modern tabloid in Europe at the time. It was a terrific paper to work for.

FG: You were on the crime beat for most of your twenty-seven years there?
AM: Oh yes, all of them.

FG: Was there any sense in 1968–69 that the 'Bible John' killings were different, or did that come later?
AM: As one murder followed another, it became clear that there was a serial killer on the loose. I don't really think there had been anyone in my time that was preying on women to that extent and killing them. There had been Peter Manuel, but he killed anybody. He was a house-breaker. This was a different kind of thing. Dancing was a big thing in those days. These women were going out and didn't come home.

They were the victims of what many people believe was a single killer. Who was looking out for his victims at Glasgow's ballrooms. It became a big story. Ordinary people were upset by the whole thing. Women began to make sure they went out with company and left with company. Bible John became this bogeyman in Scotland.

You know, mothers who would warn their kids that Bible John will get you, if you do this or that. It became a major thing if you lived in Scotland.

FG: It seems to have quickly transcended being a Glasgow story to become something else entirely. I wondered if the initial inquiry led by Joe Beattie had been too cosy with the press. Is that fair?

AM: No, I don't think so. The police realized that the press were their vehicle for getting the information to the public. I can't say it was all that cosy. They certainly wanted publicity and if you call that being cosy with the press, then yes they were.

People were phoning up the newspapers telling them they knew who Bible John was and we passed the information on to them. I suppose there were good relationships with the police, but they obviously kept things back. They had their secrets. Joe Beattie put all his eggs in the one basket. That was the sister of the last victim. He hung on every word she said. She used to take a good drink. They'd get her tanked up on booze and ask her to recollect things and all the rest of it.

He was quite certain that she remembered what she remembered. That it was all true. He just didn't stop to think that he should be looking at other things. I saw him look at photographs [of men] and say, 'that isn't him'. He thought he'd know him if he came face to face. He'd look at a photograph and say, 'oh his teeth are too long', you know? He was consumed by the whole thing.

FG: Did you know Joe Beattie?
AM: Oh, I knew him very well. He was a great guy. He'd been a fighter pilot and had risen up through the ranks in some very tough areas of Glasgow. He was a terrific guy. But as I say, as I say, he was consumed by Bible John.

FG: You were at the *Record* for so many years. Can you tell me what it was like then, after the initial inquiry and hysteria? What happened in the decades after? Is it true that Bible John was always big news, whenever a tip-off or fresh lead came in?
AM: Any possible link that came up, we were always anxious to report on it.

FG: Do you think that there really was a serial killer?
AM: I'm pretty sure there was actually. They were so close together, as well as the modus operandi and all the rest of it. Having said that, most female murder victims were strangled and often with articles of their own clothing. Because there's nothing else for [the killer] to do it with. And a lot of them are on their periods, which could have enraged the killer because he can't have his way with them.

My mind is open but I think it was one guy. It might conceivably have been two guys, but we'll never know. We'll never know. The only thing that we know in 2022 is that he's dead and has likely been dead for a good number of years.

FG: There's not going to be this cathartic moment, where the killer is unmasked. You don't believe that?
AM: No. Never.

FG: Over your very long career, was it the story that attracted the most attention, because that's what the narrative seems to be now, as if it were always a story that existed somewhat apart?
AM: No, not really. I was involved in other stories that were just as big. There was a very big story, the Glasgow Rape Case.* That affected the entire way that the police and Crown Office dealt with rape cases. So no, Bible John

---

* In 1980, a woman, invariably later referred to simply as Carol X, had been raped and assaulted after walking through an East End housing estate. The initial trial had collapsed after concerns about her capacity to give evidence. After much legal wrangling, she was granted the right to a private prosecution, only the second of its kind in Scotland during the twentieth century. Much of the media coverage of the case was later criticized for its sensationalism and aggressiveness.

wasn't the biggest. But it is the one that's remained most imprinted in people's minds to this day.

FG: Why do you think its reputation has remained so outsized, in comparison to these other crimes?

AM: Because of the nickname. That's what captured the public's imagination. A sadistic, Bible-quoting, sexual killer who was a bogeyman even to children. That's what's kept it going. I wonder if young people in their twenties would even know who Bible John was.

FG: Was it John Quinn who came up with it? I just wanted to double-check because you occasionally hear different things.

AM: I think it was, or one of the subs at the paper. John Quinn was reputed to have done so.

FG: Do you ever get sick of talking about it? Is this the story that most people ask you about, even today?

AM: I've been on television God knows how many times talking about it over the decades. People still ask me about it. You know, who do I think it was, is he dead, is he alive? The sort of questions you're asking me.

FG: There have always been these supposed prime suspects shoehorned into it. What did that make you feel at

the time: were any realistic or were you always sceptical?

AM: Yeah, there was the individual who thought his old best mate was Bible John. The guy who left the country straight after the murders and moved to Holland. That was me who went over to track him down. I knew I wasn't going to be confronted by Bible John. We did see the guy and spoke with him. We got his photograph and all that sort of thing. There was just no way he was [the killer] but there were lots of people like that.

* * *

The rest of the 1980s mostly represented a blank spot for Bible John, at least in my own searchings. I'd been particularly struck by the odd little vignette containing the long-lost friends and the story of mutual indignity and suspicion that had played out so publicly in the press. It seemed to contain so much of the Bible John myth. The giddiness and obsession of Harry Wylie, versus the outing of David Henderson, whose world must have been radically altered by the accusation of his former friend. I wondered about his life in the small Dutch town and what his neighbours must have made of the Glasgow crime reporters swooping down into their half-rural idyll. I wondered if his wife ever wavered in her conviction of her husband's immutable goodness, or whether she felt a chill when she caught sight of his face at night. I wondered what Joe Beattie had in the private files mentioned in the brief interview he'd given after the story had broken. Most of all, I began to consider if the pursuit into the depths of the Bible John mythology was doing me much good at all.

It was around the same time that I'd decided to make contact with George Puttock. Having sent a lengthy text to his mobile, I'd tried the landline number when it seemed clear enough that there wasn't going to be a response. A recently published *Daily Record* interview had brought him back into the public eye, though the piece had also mentioned his ill health (he was by now well into his eighties). It wasn't a particularly good feeling, picking up the phone to dredge up his wife's murder for what would have been the thousandth time. A gruff male voice answered the call after the second or third ring, upon which I immediately launched into my prepared speech on the book and the new angle I was trying to develop.

Puttock heard me out and there was a brief, dense pause before he responded. There was no chance, he said. I can't recall what I garbled back in response, but it was hard to shake the heavy silence when the line died a few seconds later.

JOHN MCINNES

The ancient mass of case files, witness statements and physical evidence – twenty-five boxes in total – was to be dusted off again and pored over in 1992 after an extensive collection of religious porn was discovered in a house on the fringes of Glasgow. The same story that played out in the same specific order. Just another lead that flared rapidly before fizzling out to nothing.

A year later came the announcement of the news that was to culminate in the exhumation of the body of John McInnes on the bitter, frozen morning in February 1996. There had been a semen stain left on Helen Puttock's tights, which had been preserved in storage ever since. With the rapid recent developments in forensic science, Strathclyde detectives issued a public statement, which tentatively outlined that it might now be possible to re-examine the sample using what were then pioneering techniques in genetic profiling.

Little more was released to the public until December 1995, when the news broke in the *Sunday Mail* that a freshly hand-picked team of detectives were actively investigating the Bible John case again. The new probe was to be run out of the new and expensively built Partick Police Station on Dumbarton Road, a couple of hundred yards away from the derelict old Marine building which had been emptied at the end of 1993. A four-person team began to work under the supervision of Chief Inspector Jim McEwan, sifting through the apparently endless mass of evidence from the initial inquiry and the uneven, unwieldy bulk that had accumulated in the decades since.

Two of the new team were to spend innumerable hours interviewing the detectives who had taken the initial statements, almost all of whom had long retired. Memories had frayed, which was to be expected. A quarter-century had passed full of competing impressions and recollections, personal and professional. These conversations were logged in the bulky new computers that had started to become fixtures at the dawn of the new decade. This work is often described as granular and painstaking. The list of potential suspects remained dauntingly imprecise, though it was eventually narrowed down to twelve.

The name John McInnes had begun to reoccur repeatedly in their new inquiries. Born in 1938 at home in Stonehouse, he had been raised by devout Plymouth

Brethren parents in the village, along with his brother and sister. According to several reports, the family were comfortably off rather than wealthy, and ran a moderately successful local drapery shop. His childhood was uneventful, as was those of his siblings. They'd attended the village primary school, before taking the entrance exam for Hamilton Academy. Home life was flecked with religion, with mandatory attendance at the weekly Brethren meetings at the hall on Hill Road. This particular strain of evangelical belief had flourished in the tightly knit and inward-looking Lanarkshire villages. For the most observant, the outside world was little more than a source of anxiety and disdain. From earliest childhood, McInnes was particularly close to his mother, Elizabeth, who insisted he use her maiden name Irvine as his first name, a habit which endured right up to late adolescence and beyond.

At 19, McInnes was called up for National Service, which he completed with the Scots Guards. Evidently, there was something about the experience that had chimed with the young man from the isolated Lanarkshire village, as he signed up to 45 Platoon stationed hundreds of miles south in Pirbright, Surrey, during the summer of 1957 after a brief stint working at a high-end Glasgow clothes shop. This was not the start of a glitteringly successful military career. His superiors could only remember a shy, sickly boy who'd failed to impress his instructors. After basic training, he'd been demoted to 46 Platoon's L Company and placed under the supervision of a sympathetic Lance Corporal named Gus Macdonald, who took the young recruit under his wing. Later, Macdonald recalled McInnes's awkwardness and formed the impression that he'd been deeply affected by his father's sudden death a couple of years before. The young man wasn't really much of a drinker and mostly kept himself to himself, according to his army mentor. When McInnes passed out in 1958, he gifted Macdonald a silver cigarette case with a map of the UK engraved along its front as a mark of his respect and gratitude for his support.

Not everyone from his army days was to remember McInnes with such fondness. William Sloan had slept in the next bed along in their barracks, and recalled a very different figure, a heavy drinker and sharp operator with a well-developed devious streak. In Alan Crow and Peter Samson's book, Sloan describes a night when McInnes had stayed out late drinking rather than attending to his regimental chores. The rest of them had chipped in to cover for McInnes, so he'd avoid a reprimand from their superiors. Instead of showing anything like gratitude, he simply went out again the following night. Sloan hadn't particularly liked McInnes. He thought him cold and cunning, though that's about as far as it went. McInnes was eventually discharged in 1959 and returned to Glasgow, where he took a job as a salesman for McGregor's, a furniture store on Sauchiehall Street. At first, it seemed to be a perfect fit. The shy, insular young man had blossomed, according to the testimony of Gus Macdonald who had bumped into his old charge by chance a year later. It was like meeting an entirely different person. McInnes, his regimental tie proudly on display, offered Macdonald a discount on a suite and seemed glad to see his old mentor, who was thrilled by the dramatic change.

It was the same year that McInnes met 21-year-old Ella Russell, a coalminer's daughter from Muirkirk in Ayrshire. Their courtship was brief and intense. Within months, the two were engaged. The 25-year-old McInnes was a respectable catch. Tall and charming, with a strong chin and an angular face, he had long been noted for his immaculate dress sense (and penchant for heavy, expensively tailored suits), perhaps ingrained from his childhood in the family draper's business or during his stint working in the Glasgow clothes store. Work was going well, perhaps better than well. By the time of the engagement, McInnes had taken a role as assistant manager at a different Glasgow furniture store. The couple were married at Muirkirk Parish Church on 16 March 1964 in a small Brethren ceremony attended by only the closest members of both families. The Russells had met their new son-in-law twice. The newlyweds' first child was born exactly nine months after the ceremony, on 2 December. They named the girl Lorna.

The cracks began to appear almost immediately. McInnes had grown into an increasingly hard drinker and, by the time of his marriage, a regular and perhaps compulsive gambler. Alan Crow and Peter Samson's account of these years is full of pleasingly squalid detail. Much of McInnes's social life centred around The Old Ship Inn in Stonehouse, a dour stone-fronted pub a couple of minutes from his mother's house on 26 Queen Street. The routine was simple enough. He'd arrive alone, or with his brother, Hector, for a couple of half-and-halfs: a whisky washed down with a half pint of heavy beer. Despite his overly smart attire, McInnes wasn't above inserting himself into the usual rounds of scurrilous local gossip. The wagers would then invariably begin. Usually, in the form of a game of dominoes with the disarmingly shrewd elderly afternoon crowd. The stakes were low, as these were not affluent times in the village. McInnes would often come out the worse. The other players tolerated this strange apparition, with his tales of city life and preposterous bravado. Many of them later recalled a man full of strange and alien urban ways. The daytime crowd were not particularly religious men and were amused whenever McInnes would lapse into one of his inveterate bursts of scripture.

John and Ella McInnes went into business together early on in their marriage, with a brief and ultimately disastrous foray into running a private home for the elderly out in Ayrshire. The venture almost immediately became the source of scandalized gossip, though it's unclear how much of this ever blew back into Stonehouse. There was talk that John McInnes would regularly jump into his elderly residents' beds to comfort them in times of distress, though none of them ever reported his behaviour. Much later, one of Ella's cousins corroborated this bizarre vignette to reporters. She had only been 19 at the time and had convinced herself that nothing below board was going on. The main thing she remembered was that the elderly residents would suddenly go very quiet, perhaps through fear, though she couldn't say for sure. McInnes had also borrowed £1,000 from his younger relative, though the money was never returned, presumed frittered away during a particularly dismal run of gambling losses. McInnes then took a new job at a furniture outlet in Ayr, which he started in 1968. Rumours continued to swirl around the strange and increasingly highly strung figure. There was talk that he had checked into a psychiatric hospital, possibly to dodge accusations of embezzlement from his new employers.

Amid the chaos, there were still bouts of the old salesy charm that occasionally shone through. The same cousin remembers giddy nights when McInnes would return home with groaning silver platters of food he'd convinced a local hotel to gift him and his young family. But she also recalls his increasingly red and watery stare, as well as creeping bouts of unexplained absence. One night, McInnes was pulled over for drunk driving in his distinctive green Ford Cortina. Ella, by then pregnant with their second child (who was later stillborn), was called to bail him out. Crow and Samson quote a villager who knew McInnes during the same period. His father was one of McInnes's regular gambling partners at The Old Ship Inn, who increasingly saw the strange young man as a figure of fun; a bizarre and insubstantial character who was rapidly becoming an easy mark. The old men would often wait for his arrival so they could collect a few straightforward winnings. The quoted villager mainly remembered McInnes's strange loping gait, a kind of nervous gambol, as if he were perpetually tensed on the balls of his feet.

There was another new job by the time of Patricia Docker's murder in February 1968, perhaps due to the accusations of financial impropriety that had clouded his time in Ayr. It was around this time that John and Ella McInnes separated (almost immediately after the birth of their son, Kenneth), though they weren't formally divorced until 1972. His new role was a managerial sales position at a US-based stamp-trading firm with an office in Glasgow, which McInnes could comfortably commute to by car. The honeymoon period didn't last long. McInnes was immediately clocked as a disquieting presence by his co-workers (it was later alleged that this oddness sometimes took the form of spasmodic biblical quotation). Sales meetings were generally held on Thursday nights, though McInnes's attendance record was patchy from the very beginning. He made little attempt to cover up the cause of his frequent absences. In fact, he was quite happy to attribute them to his increasingly enthusiastic excursions to the Barrowland Over-25s night.

This string of coincidences wasn't to go unnoticed by the time that Bible John hysteria reached its peak after the murder of Helen Puttock in the autumn of 1969. McInnes was picked up and brought into the Marine Division on four separate occasions during the overheated initial inquiry. Though he hadn't been picked out from any of the line-ups, neither had he been unequivocally ruled out as a suspect. This became a source of pride to the increasingly erratic McInnes, who was more than willing to talk to his pub cronies about his new-found notoriety. Some in Stonehouse even took to mockingly calling him Bible John. One villager was later quoted by the press, adamant that he had seen McInnes after his third trip to the Marine. The two had stopped in the street, while McInnes excitedly unloaded every minute and inconsequential detail of his experience in Partick.

It still isn't clear how closely McInnes was scrutinized by Joe Beattie or his team of detectives, who were being confronted by the fresh hourly crush of sightings and tip-offs. *Bible John: Hunt for a Killer* contains a brief vignette told to the authors by an anonymous Stonehouse resident who'd known McInnes from childhood. He'd turned up at her front door around December 1969 and made his way into her home. McInnes was distracted and motor-mouthed. There was something about him that seemed different, almost frightening. Something in his look and speech. She'd heard the news about his connection to the Bible John probe, which had dominated conversation and newsstands even in the relative isolation of the village. Something told her to run. She left the house and turned back, to see McInnes standing completely still in her living room, in the exact same position she'd left him. This strange scene was frozen in amber for two hours until the woman's neighbour returned and turfed McInnes out.

The next few years of his life are mostly a blank. Bible John began to recede from the newsstands and Stonehouse reverted to what it had always been. Nothing much disturbed the quietness, aside from the brief burst of activity surrounding the doomed New Town project and that surrounding the yearly summer fair. The years passed. McInnes was briefly set up in business by his mother, though his sweetshop barely lasted a year in the village. The pub visits became marathon sessions of bitterness and recrimination. Days melted into weeks. There were dark mutterings about his increasingly black depressions. On Tuesday, 29 April 1980, John McInnes visited The Old Ship Inn for his usual rounds of whisky and heavy beer. Though he didn't stay as long as normal, several regulars noted that he had drunk more than usual. The pub was busy. McInnes left and made the short walk to his mother's house on Queen Street, where he climbed up to the attic. His body was discovered the next day, just after 10.15 a.m. and was examined by a local doctor. Forty-one-year-old John McInnes had slashed his brachial artery, the thick, taught tube that runs from armpit to elbow, with a razor blade.

The suicide was registered in the nearby village of Strathhaven by Hector McInnes, while the funeral came and went a few days later, a small service attended by only the closest family. The coffin was delivered to

Stonehouse Cemetery and laid to rest in the same lot as McInnes's father. Elizabeth McInnes died in 1987 aged 91. Villagers had long spoken of a broken, disappointed woman who never quite grew to understand the life or death of her favourite son. Her coffin was placed carefully above his in the family lot. A simple line of scripture was cut into the headstone. TILL HE COME, a reference to the Resurrection and the Last Supper, as described in Corinthians.

The four-person team at Partick Police Station knew they were on to a good thing by early January 1996. John McInnes fitted neatly into so much of what they thought was known about the murders of Patricia Docker, Jemima MacDonald and Helen Puttock. There was the fact of his religious upbringing and enthusiastic attendance at the Barrowland. There was his name and the decent-enough resemblance to the various photofits and artists' impressions. He had been fond of wearing his regimental tie, a detail which had cropped up in some accounts of Helen Puttock's murder. The killings had stopped when he abruptly left his role at the stamp-trading firm without claiming his weekly expenses (colleagues said he'd mentioned a trip to Australia, though no one could say with any certainty). After weeks of deliberation, Jim McEwan's team prepared a granularly detailed report to be sent to the procurator fiscal, requesting permission to exhume the grave in Stonehouse. Detectives had even visited a long-retired and chronically ill Joe Beattie, to inform him of the news and ask him, yet again, to share his memories of the initial Helen Puttock murder inquiry The plan was to collect a DNA sample that could be checked against the stain on Helen Puttock's tights, after a genetic finger-print developed from a sample given by one of McInnes's cousins had proved an intriguingly close match. When permission came back, it was time to go public. On 27 January 1996, a spokesperson for Strathclyde Police issued a statement to the press. It merely confirmed the rumours that had already begun to swirl across news desks at Glasgow's tabloids and broadsheets alike, about a suicide out in Stonehouse whom police were increas-ingly confident was the semi-mythical Bible John.

The tabloids needed little prompting on what to do next. On 29 January, the *Daily Record* ran with a double-page spread on the dramatic new developments. Patricia Docker, Jemima MacDonald and Helen Puttock's names were brought back into circulation, though the vast majority of space remained devoted to the new prime suspect. *IS THIS BIBLE JOHN'S GRAVE? COPS COULD SOLVE A 27-YEAR-OLD MURDER RIDDLE* headlines a piece alive with gripping detail. Packs of eager reporters had already been working overtime out in Stonehouse. Two locals are quoted, speaking about the dark and sinister loner who had grown up in the shadow of a domineering mother and had turned from religion to a life lived as a 'drunken and womanising monster'. The piece lauds the efforts of the hand-picked detectives who had spent six months working tirelessly, poring over the original case files and feeding every single witness and suspect statement from the original inquiry into their state-of-the-art computer system.

George Puttock stares out from the top right of page 5. In a *Record* exclusive, the husband who lives in limbo is quoted on how he hopes he can finally achieve some sort of closure. He had been visited by detectives at his home in Berkshire, who administered a DNA test to conclusively rule out his involvement. The police needed to get the record straight, he told the paper, though he remembered the graft that had gone into the initial inquiry. If this McInnes was the man, then it would be a vindication of all the efforts that had gone before. Puttock had long remarried and was particularly concerned about the effect the news would have on his now adult children, who had been deeply traumatized by their mother's murder. Not everyone was convinced by the new suspect. A writer named Donald Simpson is quoted extensively, having just finished a book on the infamous historic murders. *Power in the Blood* was due to be published in April 1996 along with its spectacular central claim. Not only was Bible

John alive, but Simpson knew his identity and it was a Glaswegian man he'd befriended years before. Simpson had spent half a decade working on his opus and stood by every word, whatever the tests on John McInnes might reveal. It didn't matter what police managed to dig up, he knew the truth. 'Forensic science is not infallible. I have a powerful story that I still believe and the public will have to judge for themselves when it comes out. They will see it's not nonsense.'

The coming days brought the speculation to fever pitch. Another familiar mood set in, one of giddy theatricality, of the sort that had marked the press response in the aftermath of Helen Puttock's murder in 1969. The scoop centred on McInnes's identity had arrived from a young reporter at *Scotland on Sunday* named Audrey Gillan, though her involvement is rarely mentioned, even in the contemporaneous book-length accounts that deal with the McInnes saga.

Another *Daily Record* exclusive arrived the next day. BIZARRE SUICIDE OF BIBLE JOHN: MANIAC KILLED HIMSELF FOR KICKS. Though the exhumation had yet to be carried out, there was no legal reason why the papers had to hold back. Whatever other facts might emerge, McInnes was long dead and hardly able to sue for defamation. Joe Beattie is quoted in the accompanying piece, with a startling admission amid the flow of McInnes's salacious biography. It was wrong, he said, to have ever blamed all three murders on one man. 'No one ever really thought there was one man who killed three times. The cases were never really linked.' Donald Simpson also returns, still relentlessly pushing his own headline-grabbing theory. He couldn't be more certain that one man was responsible, and it wasn't John McInnes. Another crime writer, Douglas Skelton, is given space to suggest that McInnes was indeed a killer, though of one woman, rather than multiple. Instead, Bible John was likely to have been two or more men working in tandem, and could well have been responsible for up to eleven murders, rather than the three that had become synonymous with the name.

Whatever the truth, it represented a busy time for self-proclaimed experts of all stripes. A psychiatrist from Parkhead Hospital out in Glasgow's East End is quoted extensively. Dr Prem Misra presents the striking claim that the method of McInnes's suicide painted the picture of a psychopath. 'There is a possibility that he got a kick out of this. It may have given him pleasure to bleed himself to death.' The 'perversion' was exceptionally rare, the doctor continues, and they had seen only maybe four similar cases throughout their career. Another apparent medical professional closes the piece, with another equally striking and unverifiable claim. 'Intelligent, difficult to trap psychopaths like Bible John' were remorseless, impulsive and violence prone, often with unusual fetishes. If McInnes was the killer, then he might have felt satisfaction diminish with each murder. The speculation doesn't end there. 'He would want them [sic] more and more until he would go to any length to get the same kick.' He may, the piece closes, have simply killed himself in chasing 'the ultimate gory thrill'.

Patricia Docker, Jemima MacDonald and Helen Puttock don't make it much past a few cursory mentions. Each passing day brought freshly squalid revelations about the man who was to be dug up from his resting place in Stonehouse. McInnes's ex-wife Ella was tracked down to her home in Saudi Arabia, where she had moved with her third husband, a senior figure at an electronics firm. It was the press, rather than the police, who had broken news of the exhumation, he explains. They had been married for fifteen years and rarely spoke of the past, if ever. Reporters from the *Daily Record* had arrived in New Zealand, after a tip-off regarding the location of McInnes's daughter Lorna, now aged 31 and happily married. Of course, it was all a terrible shock, Lorna explained to the journalists 'from back home' who'd turned up at her door. She didn't really have all that many memories of her father and, anyway, it was all so long ago. Her brother Kenneth is also quoted from his home in Berkshire. They'd only ever really known their father briefly before their parents' divorce. He was in shock, what else could he really say (the piece is given the bold, snappy headline *I NEVER KNEW DAD WAS BIBLE JOHN*).

It seemed as if there was no end to the new cast of characters arriving on set from the long-forgotten past. One of McInnes's old bosses appears, to say how unsurprised he was at the news. In fact, he had long suspected his fastidious, if terminally unreliable one-time employee of being the infamous Barrowland serial murderer (though police sources had been keen to stress that the McInnes exhumation was related to the Helen Puttock murder alone, the press still had no intention of dropping the Bible John angle). It was the likeness, the man explains, as well as the lapses into biblical quotation that he could remember vividly to this day. A succession of ex-drinking partners and village worthies make their appearance to say a few revealing words about the desperate loner they'd once known. George Puttock returned, this time in a loudly heralded series of exclusives with the *Daily Record*. The new interview went further than any that had gone before. The now 55-year-old Puttock had long ago remarried and moved back to Berkshire. He explained that he had been consumed by the case, even launching his own investigation in the years following Helen's murder. For a long time, he had been convinced that Peter Sutcliffe, the so-called 'Yorkshire Ripper', was responsible, having linked him to the place and time. Whatever else, there had been decades of torment, the pain and anger of losing his wife. It ran so deep that he had never visited her grave, he told reporters. Though detectives had come to his door to take a DNA test, the results had quickly deleted the notion that he could still be a suspect. The next page carries a photo of George Puttock kneeling by his ex-wife's headstone in Lambhill Cemetery on the northern fringes of Glasgow. The *Record* had brought him there for an unmissable photo opportunity. One can almost feel the bitter March morning through the picture, with the snow-covered Campsies in the background, as Puttock gingerly squats side-on with a purple puffer jacket covering his smart dark green suit.

On the next page is a small photo of a young man, wearing a smile and a well-kept mullet. It is 31-year-old David Puttock, who was 5 when his mother was murdered. He would have killed the killer, no questions asked. He would have wanted him to experience the same pain his mother had. What hurt is that he didn't know her better and he was angry at himself that he'd never visited Scotland to try and find out more. He found that difficult to cope with, as if he had failed somehow. He still wanted to know why she was killed. Was it because the killer had been sick, or ill? He had needed to see him alive, so he could understand why. But there was no arrest, no trial.

It was like he didn't exist. He was going to make the trip soon, to finally visit her grave for the first time. He had never been able to let her memory go. 'I don't want her to be forgotten and I will tell my children what happened to their gran. On every birthday I think about her. I get distant and I think what it would be like if she was still here. Because of that bastard it is something I'll never know.'

News of the exhumation and the accompanying photograph of John McInnes had sent police phone lines into a fresh meltdown. The familiar story played out, yet again. Calls arrived from dozens of women who were convinced they'd danced with him in the late 1960s. They said that they could clearly remember the figure almost thirty years on. An anonymous detective told reporters how incredible it was that the same women hadn't come forward at the time. Maybe they'd been too young or frightened, the unnamed source speculates. A senior figure at Strathclyde Police was then wheeled out to stress how seriously this new burst of information was being treated, with the utmost carefulness and precision. George Puttock appeared again the next day, in yet another Scottish exclusive tucked into page 5 of the *Daily Record*. This time the tabloid's photographers had lined up Puttock with a copy of the paper in his hands, with the edition that had John McInnes's face plastered across it. The new piece contained a number of minor new revelations. Puttock explained how he'd suffered a heart attack when police had informed him of the new probe into his ex-wife's murder. His explanation was that it would force him to again 'fight to defend her honour'. The thing that had always hurt the most was that 'people made her out to be a tart ... I want people to know what Helen really was – a terrific mum and a vivacious girl.'

Puttock had spent two years fighting a legal battle against Granada TV after the channel had aired an episode on Helen Puttock's murder as part of their *In Suspicious Circumstances* series, which had re-enacted the killing. The Broadcasting Complaints Commission had upheld George Puttock's complaint, after ruling that it constituted an unwarranted infringement of privacy. The programme's makers had also allegedly neglected to give Puttock a right of reply and that he should have been offered the chance of an advance screening. It's impossible now to know precisely what was alleged in the programme, though it had challenged Puttock's long-standing account of the night of his wife's murder. The *Herald* responded to the 1994 ruling with a short piece relaying his response to a programme which he thought painted him as a liar and misrepresented his Helen. The lawsuit is referenced in the new *Daily Record* interview, where Puttock goes on to say how it contributed to the heart attack he'd suffered after reaching an out-of-court settlement with Granada. It was soon after this that detectives had arrived at his door for the DNA sample. He knew, he says, that 'the innuendos would come out again' and he simply couldn't take it. No, he hadn't liked his Helen going out with her friends, but there was nothing to be done about it. When it came to John McInnes, he was just glad that the killer was caught and even more relieved that he wasn't alive, though he couldn't deny he was angry that there'd be no real punishment.

On the morning of the exhumation, the same paper ran a prepared double-page spread with Dr Marie Cassidy, the forensic pathologist who was to be in charge of removing McInnes's coffin from its resting place. The piece is accompanied by a photograph of a slightly bemused-looking blonde woman in a sharp grey suit, who has clearly been asked to pose in her lab with a microscope. She confirmed that this would be her second exhumation and there would be no doubt once the appropriate tests had been undertaken. And no, she wasn't squeamish about the task ahead of her. Death is her job, she explains. It was a pretty straightforward task, but it was a particularly fascinating case and she was delighted to be involved.

A special notice had been issued, telling any morbidly curious members of the public to stay away from the cemetery on the morning of 1 February. The villagers themselves didn't need to be told. There had been discomfort ever since the news had broken, at the swarm of reporters and strange visitors that had begun to make their way to Stonehouse. Some members of the press had spent the previous night camping outside the cemetery, though they quickly lost their position in the sixty-strong crowd of reporters that had appeared by first light, as if by magic, while a helicopter whined overhead, having been rented by one the Glasgow tabloids. One neighbouring farmer had turned up with a video camera, but the police were more concerned with the three strangers – two middle-aged women and a thickly bearded, flat-cap-clad man with horn-rimmed glasses – who had turned up at the gates and initially refused to identify themselves. Several of the half-frozen reporters began to place bets to kill the time. Were they members of the McInnes family, or representatives from some obscure religious group, looking to drum up a bit of free publicity?

Eventually, the man stood up to hold an impromptu press conference. Sean O'Farraig, 59 years old, had been a professional psychic for many years before taking his place as the head of the Glasgow Psychic Centre. After observing the dig with his two fellow clairvoyants, he was happy to publicly state their unwavering opposition to the plans. He had been in contact with the ghost of Helen

Puttock for over twenty years and she had explicitly told him that this was not the man who had killed her. Instead, the murderer was still alive and living in Motherwell and had strong links to education. His colleague, Anne Ayre, had a slightly different take on McInnes. She was sure beyond doubt that he had killed, perhaps multiple times, though he wasn't Bible John. 'His problems,' she told reporters, 'started as a teenager [when] he had a lot of sexual hang-ups.' She continued that he'd had a friend 'more evil than him' and had been rejected by this same man. And she was convinced that it was this rejection that had led to his suicide.

These representatives from Glasgow's supernatural order weren't the only ones with complaints about the exhumation, which was beginning to become a national debating point. Just under a week later, the Labour MP for Dundee East offered his opinion that the dig represented a catastrophic waste of public money. Strathclyde Police issued a statement strongly rebutting the claim, before the Conservative's Scottish Chairman issued a withering public rebuke. The police did a wonderful job and should not be criticized. Indeed, 'they deserved public support rather than carping from mean-minded politicians'. Despite the intensity of the press coverage, not every write-up was a glowing endorsement of the exhumation, even in the tabloids. Joan McAlpine wrote in her

Daily Record column – the paper which had so aggres-
sively dominated Bible John coverage over the decades –
that even 'the raising of Lazarus never caused this fuss'.
For years, Bible John had haunted every dancehall in
Scotland. 'He was the weird guy on every housing scheme.
As children we were convinced he lived up the road. Now
the bogeyman is exposed as a pathetic pile of bones.'

As the weeks passed, the initial frenzy abated just as it
had done with every other Bible John story before it, even
if there was still the sense – a burgeoning belief – that
John McInnes still represented something different. And
there were other murders to jostle with Bible John for
attention, a fact as true in the mid-1990s as it had been
almost thirty years before. There had been a breakthrough in another historic murder case from 1986,
where a 16-year-old girl from Greenock had been killed
after a night spent dancing at a local disco. The new suspect was already facing another murder charge and
couldn't be named for legal reasons. Another teenage girl
had recently been killed in Kilmarnock and the *Daily
Record* devoted a jubilant front page to an underworld
pledge that the alleged culprit was unlikely to get out of
jail alive, as his killing had already been ordered in
revenge.

The process of checking the DNA samples against the
stain on Helen Puttock's tights was initially capped at

three weeks by buoyant senior figures at Strathclyde Police. While some accounts have stressed how professionally and clinically the evidence had been stored in late 1969, others have raised significant doubt. In *Chasing Killers*, Joe Jackson writes about an era where physical evidence, stained clothing or otherwise, was poorly stored in plastic bags, and could often ferment. He notes how consulting scientists would simply ask detectives to dry the items out, which was usually achieved by draping them out over boiler-room pipes in the office. Though he couldn't say for certain when it came to Helen Puttock's clothing, he couldn't see it being treated with the requisite care needed for a clear DNA comparison (it was later reported that the samples taken had in fact been badly degraded after years of exposure underground). Weeks quickly turned into months and experts were eventually called in from the University of Cambridge to assist in compiling the report, who in turn brought in help from the Institute of Medicine in Berlin.

The pressure had long begun to mount, political and otherwise. Reputations had been staked and staked hard on McInnes being Bible John. Books were already being written with barely conceivable haste now the mystery was deemed to be nearing its end. The delay caused nerves to fray and tempers with them. The months continued to pass. There was little else to do but wait and doubt began to flourish in the shadow of the long silence. Jeannie Williams was dragged back into the public eye, though she was increasingly certain that McInnes wasn't the man from the taxi the night her sister had been killed. In early July 1996, the Crown Office finally issued a public statement on the exhumation of John McInnes and the long, painstaking scientific process that had followed it. Despite the expense (the *Herald* reported that the inquiry had cost nearly £1 million) and controversy, despite the weight of column inches and press attention, the results had failed to link John McInnes to the semen stain found on Helen Puttock's clothing.

The backlash was swift. One Labour MP demanded a full public apology to the McInnes family, who had found themselves placed under months of intense suspicion and scrutiny. Another opined that while the police had a duty to investigate historic murder cases, the debacle seemed to set a precedent on how not to go about it. The *Herald* also noted that though the public statement issued from the Crown Office had been unusually detailed, it made no mention of how one of the most sensitive investigations undertaken by a Scottish police force had been so comprehensively leaked to the media.

THE GRAVE

I caught the Caledonian Sleeper from Euston to Glasgow Central in late February 2022. It was stuffy on the train and I didn't sleep particularly well in my thin little bunk-bed, so I switched the overhead light on in the early hours to reread the notes I'd made on John McInnes and the circus that surrounded his exhumation, as well as the string of failures that had followed it.

It was my first trip of the year up to Scotland and I'd come with a couple of specific thoughts in mind. It had been a while since I'd visited my friends dotted around Glasgow, too long in fact, and I was keen to catch up and see how the long winter months were treating them. Mostly though, I had come to visit Stonehouse, the Lanarkshire village that had filled my reading and research for so many weeks. To have such a clearly defined mental picture of a place you've never visited is an odd thing, a vivid jumble of old news reports and photographs, and whatever might be gleaned from slightly out-of-date Google Street View imagery. Having checked into my hotel, a reassuringly bland newbuild a few minutes' walk from the station, I took to my phone to find the quickest route by public transport.

The first train to Motherwell was cancelled, then the second too. Finally, there was the chance of a train near enough to Larkhall, where I was to change for the 254 bus which ran through to Stonehouse. Naturally, when the time came, I managed to miss the connection, though it wasn't clear if the bus had been early or just hadn't arrived at all. There was plenty of time to contemplate this deep philosophical axiom as I sheltered from the rain under the bus stop.

Around 45 minutes later, I presented my change to the driver and took my seat on the near-empty bus. We weaved through a succession of thin country roads, bordered by sodden fields and emancipated hedgerows. After around twenty minutes the bus pulled up in the centre of the village by a small Spar newsagent's and a succession of low, rain-streaked stone buildings. The streets were empty, save for a couple of pensioners wrapped tightly in their waterproofs, carrying a few bags of shopping. I pulled out my phone and tapped at the greasy screen until the map popped up directing me to the cemetery where

John McInnes and his mother had been quietly returned to their burial place in the summer of 1996.

I made my way along a deserted residential road, passing a boarded-up amusement arcade and a dark, heavy-looking church. It wasn't long before the pavement gave way to a bare country road that cleaved through the middle of several damp fields. Though the rain had stopped, the wind had re-doubled and I stopped under a severe concrete underpass to fish another jumper from my rucksack.

Quarter of a mile or so later, I arrived at the gates of Stonehouse Cemetery, a neat little country graveyard surrounded by a few rows of mid-2000s executive homes. A small printed-out sign tied to a lamppost proclaimed that SAID WAS HERE (BUT YOU'D NEVER KNOW IT BECAUSE SHE TOOK HER CIGARETTE BUTTS HOME). It had just gone 12.20 when I walked in and began to trace the gravel paths underfoot. The sky had turned into a blurred marbly grey, undercut with a few confused streaks of blue. The cold provoked a few involuntary shivers and there was the unmistakable sense of being entirely alone.

It was hard to imagine the scrum of reporters and officials who had spent the agonizingly bitter morning here in February 1996, as I made my way along the rows of modest headstones. I quickly found a couple of McInneses, though they weren't the right family. They had died early in the 1960s and 1970s respectively. Though it felt ridiculous, I couldn't quite shake the sudden feeling that I was being watched. It wasn't long before the rain picked back up, as I steeled myself for another loop of the burial ground.

THE PATHOLOGIST

A couple of months after my trip to Stonehouse, I'd made my way back up to Glasgow for another few weeks' worth of researching and reporting. It was the start of an intensely warm, bright spring, which I found just as unexpected and disorientating as I do every year, after the long, bitter winter months. The first fortnight went past quietly enough, as I split my time between the *Daily Record* office and a new perch on the fifth floor of the Mitchell Library, poring through box after box of the same old brittle microfilm, peering closer and closer at the same jumble of old news stories and features, swimming in a pool of gaudy adverts for long-forgotten and discontinued products.

John McInnes had become just another frustrating, compelling addition to add to the already cluttered mess of false starts and dead ends underpinning the entire Bible John mythology. I knew this feeling well enough by then.

Piles of loose notes and tattered, ugly paperbacks littered my desk as I waded through them for the next illuminating detail, the next jolt of revulsion or pity to keep me going in the stuffy library, as the sun blared down outside. Some of the more recent accounts ignore McInnes entirely, apart from the occasional brief aside which might mention the dramatic winter morning in Stonehouse, back in the mid-1990s. I wonder about this silence. Does it stem from embarrassment or simply from the lack of space given over by whichever editor has commissioned the brief recap, designed to hoover up as much easy attention as possible before moving on to fresher, more contemporary violence?

I'd wanted to speak with Dr Marie Cassidy for a year, at least. Something always seemed to come up for one or other of us, whenever we'd set a date. There would be some distraction; an unavoidable conference or short-notice trip out of town. In late 2020, I'd read a series of interviews after the publication of her book, *Beyond the Tape*, which charted the course of a long and distinguished career as a forensic pathologist. Cassidy always came across well, bereft of pomposity and always ready with a quick aside. Born in 1959 to an Irish Catholic family in Glasgow, she was educated by nuns who were incredulous when she'd decided to choose a career in medicine. She qualified as a forensic pathologist in 1985 and spent thirteen years based in Glasgow University's Department of Forensic Medicine and Science. Her duties were varied and included investigating unnatural deaths and suicides right through to gangland hits and every other conceivable form of murder.

Disillusionment with life in Scotland had set in by the late 1990s. The department was in flux and Cassidy had little interest in the same stale office politics. In 1998, she moved to Dublin with her young family to take up a role in Ireland. In 2003, she was promoted to become the first female State Pathologist of Ireland, a role she retired from in 2018, before writing her memoirs. To her, the exhumation of John McInnes was just another working day, she told me from her home just outside London, when we finally spoke on the phone in early May 2022. Cassidy was, as I'd expected, a humorous and resolutely professional interviewee and repeatedly wanted to stress her limited role in the John McInnes saga, though she was happy to speak in detail about exactly what it had entailed.

Our conversation has been edited for length and clarity.

Francisco Garcia: I wonder if we could talk about the day of the exhumation itself. Your own recollections of it, if that would be OK?

Marie Cassidy: It was really just another day to me really. Well, it was unusual in the sense that [one] didn't do that many exhumations. I'm afraid that I'm not a deep thinker. I just thought, 'Well, this is another job.' And that's fine, I was happy to just get on with it. I didn't realize it was going to grow the legs it did.

As you know, [Bible John] has become like the Loch Ness Monster. It's a myth, which in this case dominates the Glasgow and Lanarkshire area.

FG: Could you talk me through the morning and what it was like?

MC: I wasn't living too far from there at the time. I was in Blackwood, just a few miles down the road in an old country estate which had been converted into flats. It really wasn't too far for me to go. But as usual with these exhumations, it was the wrong time to be doing it. You're talking about digging through ground in Lanarkshire in February. It's not ideal because the ground is so hard. And for some reason, people have it in their mind that it has to be done at the crack of dawn. I've never ever understood anything being done at the crack of dawn. I'm afraid I'm not at my best then.

But that's what always seems to be the case. I think it's maybe because in the olden days, they wanted to get in and out before anyone noticed, you know? So as not to upset people too much, as the graveyard was being disturbed. But it wasn't like that with [McInnes] unfortunately. Everybody knew what was about to happen, that it was imminent. It wouldn't have mattered what time they started. It would have gotten out anyway. People would have flocked to it. Journalists would have flocked to it. And I guess that's what happened.

I didn't see too much of it. After I'd arrived, I was immediately escorted to the tent area which was covering the graves. We then put our coveralls on. I spent most of my time away from the media frenzy that was going on somewhere behind me. Over the years, I've always been like that. You don't want to be distracted by people in and around the area. They don't have a part to play. I've always been very good at screening that out. I never really pay any attention to it, particularly cameras and whatever else might be there.

I worked in Ireland for so long, where everything was under scrutiny. Sometimes there would even be a camera over your shoulder. You learn to just blank it out, you know? Whatever it is they're up to. Just let me get on with my job. That day was the same. Yes I was there, but I only had a very small part really in the whole procedure. I was only there to safeguard the Crown side of it, as they'd made the decision to do the exhumation. And of course, they needed a forensic pathologist to oversee it, so no one could have any complaints about what was done and what wasn't done.

My role was maybe more that of an observer to begin with. And then I suppose it was really as a technician. I wasn't there to do a postmortem examination. No, I was there to gather the material that would be necessary for a DNA examination. These exhumations are often working within very strict parameters. Once you get permission to exhume a body, you need to be very careful that you only do what you've legally been allowed to do. I wasn't there to examine the body or make any comments on it. I was there, as I say, almost more as a technician than a pathologist. It was just to make sure we got the material that we thought would be useful for DNA analysis.

FG: There were such high expectations that this DNA was about to solve this – even then – incredibly high-profile and historic series of murders. Was this something you felt at the time, or did you really manage to block that noise out entirely?

MC: I think in retrospect we probably jumped the gun a bit. Although the analysis and techniques had come on leaps and bounds since we started using and utilizing them as part of our tool kit, it obviously wasn't just quite there. I suppose if we had looked at it long and hard, we would have seen that there were a lot of misses as well as hits when you're dealing with very old material. And it was very old at that time. Maybe, I don't even know if you would be able to get a better result nowadays. But they probably weren't quite there yet. There were always going to be question marks over how reliable the results were going to be, or were.

FG: And there was never a sense of pressure when this was all going on?
MC: No, it really was removed from what I'd normally be doing. If I'd been there in my capacity as a forensic pathologist and had been there to examine the body closely, for anything that might have been of interest. Well, that would have been different. There would have been a pressure on me then. But because I was dealing with something that would be analysed in the lab, the only pressure I felt was in getting the right samples. And when it came to the analysis, it didn't have anything to do with me at all. I mean, it made no odds to me whether it worked or didn't work. That was someone else's area of expertise. It's certainly not mine. And so I didn't feel any great pressure on what the results were going to be. I was just there to hopefully get the right material, or enough of the right material, for the analysis.

FG: What about the challenge of the plot itself, and the fact that John McInnes was below his mother's casket?

MC: There was one below and one above him. When it comes down to it, you have to be very very careful. We had to make sure we didn't unnecessarily disturb the other bodies. Yes, we had to remove the first one [the coffin of McInnes's mother]. We were hoping against all odds that the coffins hadn't deteriorated, you know. You never know until you start going in. You never know how robust these coffins are going to be. You never know if they're going to have withstood the test of time. In the long run, of course, you expect them to collapse and dis-integrate, as the bodies (naturally) begin to collapse and disintegrate internally.

But that's not much use when you're excavating these graves, because you really don't want to be getting into a situation where there is a question mark, even down to whether you are even dealing with the right body. We were lucky from that point of view that the top coffin was intact. So we knew there wasn't going to be any of what we call the commingling of remains. His coffin was fairly intact, too. So again, there wasn't any possibility of someone saying, 'What happens if it's the body below?' or something like that. There are all things you have to be aware of. And that was my role. To make sure whatever samples were taken, there couldn't be a question mark over where it came from or who it came from.

FG: I wanted to ask something else. It's a more general question and it might sound stupid. Would you have been aware of Bible John when you were growing up in Glasgow?

MC: Oh yeah. I mean, think about it, there's not that many serial killers in the Glasgow and Strathclyde area. There was that guy before [Bible John]; what was his name?

FG: Peter Manuel?

MC: Yeah. I mean we knew of Bible John, but I didn't know the ins and outs of it. I didn't know much about the background of the women who were supposed to have been killed by this Bible John. But we did know that there had been several women who had been killed by a man, so yes we knew about it. But did we pay much heed? No, not really.

I can't say I lost sleep over it as a teenager going into the centre of Glasgow. In my day it was discotheques. It never really crossed my mind that I'd come across [this figure] who would come and do me harm.

As far as I was concerned, that was the past anyway.

**FG: There were so many people who became associ-
ated with the case. This gallery of terrible killers who
people were so determined to fit into the Bible John
story. Peter Manuel and so many others. But even now,
the 'mystery' persists. Do you remember much about the
media coverage after the exhumation, and what happened when it was increasingly clear that the legend
hadn't been solved at all?**

MC: To be honest, not really. It was one of those things,
maybe because it was an old case (or a cold case, I
suppose) where, well … Glasgow was always so full
and busy with 'warm cases'. It was around that time
[in the mid-1990s] that it started becoming known as
the murder capital. We were extremely busy with all of
these cases … the exhumation and Bible John were just
more things I didn't have time to dwell on. The murders kept coming in.

Glasgow has gone through waves of activity. It had
been the European City of Culture [in 1990] and you
were meant to think that everything was lovely and rosy.
But if you look at the homicide figures, we were extremely
busy. And so [McInnes] was just a cold case. It wasn't
something that I was going to have any other input into.
Other than to say, yes I was there and yes, I oversaw the
excavation. I retrieved the bone that was sent for DNA

analysis. There were other people there who were involved and who were also there to make sure everything was done by the book.

We had to call in the dentist who was going to look at McInnes because Bible John had allegedly left a bite mark on one of the women. Again, I had nothing to do with any of that. That was somebody else, another expert coming in to oversee that part of things.

FG: There was always violence, and murder, for you to attend to. And at root, these were murders like any other. But then again, I suppose that isn't really entirely true because Bible John had become this mythical entity by that point. In fact, that had been the case for a very long time, even by 1996.

MC: People like to big up their part in it all. They like to think that they were the most important person. That they were the most important person involved in it. Unfortunately, people do embellish things, you know? A great deal. I don't come from that school of forensic pathology. I just say look, this is the limit of my expertise. And that there's a lot of other clever people doing a lot of clever things. And I'm quite happy to bow to other people's expertise. I really don't have a problem with that at all.

FG: And there are limits to this, right? That the science is such a gift and such an immensely valuable tool, but it isn't some kind of strange and infallible magic. It's not like the kind of thing seen on TV or in films, where the scientists show up to the murder scene and wave a wand about until they spot a neatly packaged little pool of the killer's DNA on a door handle or something.

MC: I think that's maybe some of the problem. That people get an idea of someone's role from how things are represented in films and television programmes. You know, it can't just be a pathologist, they have to be a scientist as well. They have to be the police officer, too. They have to play these multiple roles to make that story work.

Whereas the sad fact of life is that there are lots and lots of people involved in every case. And we all do our own little bit. And then, hopefully, someone is able to put the jigsaw together and make the fuller picture. So, maybe in the olden days there might have been sort of half a dozen experts, but today that number is up in the hundreds. The sad fact is that people don't appreciate that.

***

I'd visited Lambhill Cemetery a few months before my dismal search for John McInnes in Stonehouse. There was a very different kind of day breaking when I set off from my battered B&B at the top of Garnethill, a few yards from the Glasgow School of Art. A crisp November morning which spread out under a bright grey sky that seemed to promise frost rather than rain.

My phone told me it would take just under an hour and a half to drift up on foot through Maryhill and beyond, right up to the stolid Victorian cemetery where Helen Puttock had been buried in 1969. The canal pathway up to Maryhill Locks was dotted with cyclists and Saturday morning walkers wrapped in fleeces and sturdy waterproofs. Children stared into the mucky dark blue water or clasped their parents' hands in silence. At one point the path became blocked by a fence next to a reinforced plywood board emblazoned with a notice for the housing developer Balfour Beatty. The No ACCESS FOR UNAUTHORIZED PERSONS sign was scrawled over with thick black permanent marker. KNOW YOUR WORTH, read the gnomic new proclamation.

It was still bright by the time I arrived at the front gate of the cemetery. This was the first time I'd met Audrey Gillan, though we'd spoken on the phone for a while a few months before. The former *Guardian* reporter had made contact the previous summer, having become aware that I was writing this book through a mutual friend of ours. Few people or journalists know the ins and outs of the Bible John saga as well as Gillan, who had broken the story of McInnes's identity as a young reporter back in the mid-1990s. Almost quarter of a century on, she'd recently started working on her own new project, a podcast re-examining her connection to Bible John and the McInnes scoop that had caused such consternation and excitement in the Scottish press.

The afternoon sun was already starting to weaken when we met by a cluster of graves at the north end of the cemetery. To the north-west lay the Campsies, the range of gentle rolling hills slightly obscured by a row of low red-brick houses in the more immediate foreground. As we began to chat, our feet angled away from the main path to a place where the ground was firm and slightly spongy under foot. Our phone screens both showed the same image: the photo of George Puttock kneeling beside Helen Puttock's grave in early 1996. An hour passed as we tried to orientate ourselves using the position of the snow-covered hills in the background.

We walked up and down several rows of neat and well-tended graves with little success. Perhaps the newish-looking houses to our left were a red herring that had thrown us off, or maybe we weren't even in the right section of the cemetery at all. These and many other justifications started to feel increasingly seductive as the sun began to set and the cold to descend in earnest. After another quarter of an hour or so of fruitless searching, we made the decision to call it a night and acknowledge something to ourselves; that we just weren't going to find Helen Puttock that day. On the walk back to Maryhill, we spoke about Bible John and a couple of the more outlandish figures and theories surrounding the mythology. Talking with Audrey immediately felt like a return to dry land, after a couple of months spent splashing in the deep strange waters of often-addled speculation. She was funny, dry and precisely to the point on the things she knew and the other things she didn't. Back at the flat she'd been staying in, we settled down to some dinner and let the conversation drift to other topics.

It was around seven when I left to meet some friends at a pub in the West End. It already felt like a long day, and I was starting to feel tired and had to strain a bit to watch my footing on the slick ice under foot, which had silently spread across the city in the time I'd been inside. I wondered what would have happened if the afternoon had played out differently. If we'd found Helen Puttock's grave rather than abandoning the search as the dark drew in. Before setting out that morning, I suppose I'd have dignified the search by explaining that it had something to do with respect for the woman whose murder I'd already spent so much time reading and writing about. That it would be a recognition of her and the reality of the crimes which had so long ago been swallowed up and digested into urban folklore. Perhaps, I thought, there was something fitting in my inability to locate her graveside. Just another false start to add to the growing collection and another way in which the facts of the past refused to conform to the desires of the present. Another layer of unreality to pull tight and close over all the other failures that had gone before.

THE PLAY

I first came across Paul Harrison in the summer of 2018. It was early on in my initial reporting, at that frenetic period in the process of putting together any story when every new lead feels brilliantly alive with possibility, or at least a certain enjoyable novelty. When the rapidly accumulating pile of books and papers might occasionally strike me as a hearty challenge rather than a bitter endurance test. It is often a greedy period, whatever the subject matter. Greed for material and greed for other people's time. I can recall ordering every book I could find that made even cursory mention of Bible John, however surreal their angle, or whatever their reviews might have warned. The paperbacks kept arriving during those weeks, some brand new and others battered with age, or yellowed from second-hand cigarette smoke (these reeking little monuments to another person's dormant or long-forgotten obsession were the ones I tended to enjoy the best).

I'd sent emails and Facebook message requests with what I liked to think was remorseless diligence, to academics and ex-police officers who would have well remembered Bible John and Joe Beattie's crusade to catch the killer. Some of these messages were answered and many others ignored. One prompt reply – perhaps the promptest – had come from Paul Harrison, author of *Dancing with the Devil: The Bible John Murders*, which had been released by an obscure publisher in 2013 to a few polite notices in the Scottish press. The *Daily Record* had briefly covered the book and its incendiary central claim: that the mythical Bible John was an unnamed Glaswegian police officer, now long retired and living in a remote corner of the Highlands.

This was no wild accusation, designed to drum up anything as vulgar as a few cheap headlines. Harrison – a prolific and moderately successful true crime writer, as well as a vastly decorated former police officer – explained to the paper how he'd spent years researching the case, which he'd never quite been able to shake. His reporting had run deep, far deeper than the dilettantes who had gone before, who had simply repeated the same old lazy assumptions and pointed to the same threadbare gallery of implausible or debunked leading suspects. It was, he writes in the book's introduction, 'a long, often dangerous journey [and] I have used every ounce of my investigative training and skills to delve … into the matter'. But Strathclyde Police hadn't wanted to know about the results of Harrison's investigation. Instead, he had been met with an orchestrated campaign of silence and hostility from Scotland's largest and most notorious police force.

Perhaps most impressively of all, he had managed to befriend and extensively interview both Joe Beattie and Jeannie Williams before their deaths in 2000 and 2010 respectively. Though Beattie wasn't in the best of health, he had taken a liking to Harrison and the two had met many times over the years. The same was true of his relationship with Jeannie Williams, who he refers to as Jeannie McLachlan. Though it was hard for Beattie to hear the mass of evidence against one of his own, it hadn't come as the most terrible or unseen of surprises. In Harrison's telling, it was Beattie's own belated suspicions against his fellow officers back in the early 1970s that had seen the inquiry dismantled. Harrison traces a vast and subtle conspiracy that culminated with Bible John slipping through the net. A plot which originated at and spread across the most senior levels of Glasgow's police force.

All of this makes for compelling reading, despite Harrison's scattergun prose. Though perhaps this is a churlish

WE ALL GO INTO THE DARK

gripe, considering the book's explosive content. Harrison explains how Jeannie Williams had told him that she'd seen the killer during one of the innumerable visits she'd made to the Marine. Having pointed at the man, Beattie had immediately dismissed it out of hand, as she'd gestured at one of his own detectives. Despite compiling an inches' thick dossier of research, Harrison thought it strange that the police had never responded to his earnest offers of help, considering his own uniquely garlanded career, including stints as an undercover football hooligan and a royal protection officer, and his status as the youngest sergeant in British policing history.

Most impressively, Harrison was also one of the first figures from British law enforcement to train at the FBI's legendary Behavioral Science Unit at Quantico, Virginia, and he was more than happy to use some of his carefully sharpened investigative prowess to profile Bible John. The killer would now be a married man with children and strong links to religion. Most chillingly of all, it was almost certain that he wouldn't have stopped killing in 1969. It was a matter of urgency, Harrison told reporters, to investigate several open murder case files across the Highlands. The man he believed to be Bible John had moved there soon after taking early retirement in the early 1970s. Only legal restraints were stopping Harrison from naming the killer, though he was still waiting with forlorn patience for the police to make contact and collaborate with his investigation. What he wanted most of all, he told the *Daily Record*, was 'justice for the families of the women he killed ... and for Joe Beattie. He was a brilliant detective who wouldn't accept [that] he couldn't close that case.'

I'd read *Dancing with the Devil* in two or three delighted sittings, punctured by bouts of increasingly wide-eyed astonishment. It was hard to know precisely what to make of it. Clearly Harrison had committed to his research. There were a few interesting factual points made about Glasgow in the 1960s and the ways it did and didn't change throughout the course of the decade. Its violence and its portrayal in the papers of the day. Mostly, it was impossible not to be struck by the book's incredible levels of access to the most important figures at the heart of the Bible John saga, ranging from several famously taciturn real-life characters to a cluster of alarmingly eloquent unnamed sources. Both Jeannie Williams and Joe Beattie lapse into paragraph- and sometimes page-long soliloquies, which remarkably always seem to exactly confirm Harrison's own hypothesis. Here is his Jeannie Williams on the suspicion she'd felt radiating from many of the officers and detectives from the Marine.

There was animosity against me, especially when Joe had officers moved off the inquiry because of issues of trust. I never fully knew what he meant but I did know that he believed that too much gossip and information was being leaked out from the investigation to the press and elsewhere. It didn't help that I felt concerned about the way some of the [officers] were speaking and [sic] treating me. More than once I was referred to as a prostitute and others would ask what I was doing later, inviting me out for a drink and a bit of fun! That wasn't me at all, I wasn't like that, it really hurt that I lost my sister to a murderer, yet some police thought it was okay to put me down and dismiss me as though I was a worthless drunk who had manipulated a situation for my own needs.

This sort of thing goes on for a number of paragraphs before eventually petering out. As soon as I'd finished the book, I knew I had to speak with Harrison, the distinguished profiler and the confidant of Joe Beattie's last years. In June 2018 we'd exchanged a brief flurry of emails. I was keen to speak about his remarkable book, whenever he might have a minute. Our diaries never did manage to align that summer. Harrison told me he was writing a feature of his own and was in the middle of a 'serial killer speaking tour' across the UK, though he assured me he'd email to discuss more on his return home. No message ever arrived. I soon forgot about our brief exchange. My original piece on Bible John was filed and life moved on. It was just over a year later when the first news reports broke in the national press, illustrated by pictures of a familiar-looking middle-aged man in rimmed glasses and a loud tartan waistcoat.

There was sadly one major issue with Paul Harrison, esteemed true crime writer, criminal profiler and Bible John authority. He had made almost everything up, from the pages of his titanic bibliography right through to the contents of his glittering and pages-long CV. Britain's self-appointed serial-killer hunter had been outed as a fraud of astonishing longevity and brazenness. The collapse of his intricate, if not particularly guileful, web of falsehoods was as sudden as it was total. A journalist from the *Sun* had attended one of Harrison's sold-out talks at a theatre in Newcastle and was instantly transfixed by the stream of fantastical nonsense pouring out of the middle-aged Cumbrian on stage.

None of the subsequently published revelations came as much of a surprise after reading his contribution to the Bible John cottage industry. No, the FBI hadn't invited a low-ranking and undistinguished police officer to train at Quantico (among the wreckage of his persona was one verifiable fact: Harrison had indeed pounded pavements in Kettering for a brief period in the 1990s). No, Peter Sutcliffe had never expressed terror in Harrison's presence (the story had been repeated so often on stage that word had even reached the killer in the high-security confines of HMP Frankland). And there was no verifiable suggestion that he'd ever so much as exchanged messages with either Joe Beattie or Jeannie Williams. His latest book was immediately pulled from sale and Harrison was sufficiently cowed to publish a brief and rapidly deleted apology on his Facebook page, which blamed his publishers and several other dark forces for the series of uncovered 'embellishments' and sensational claims.

While Bible John was little more than a footnote in Paul Harrison's private solar system of deceit, the more I thought about it, the more it seemed to make its own kind of lopsided sense. By 2013 the facts of the story, as they were, had long ago receded into the past. I thought of the news stories published to herald Harrison's Bible John book and the evident absurdity spelled out so vividly on almost every page. For the papers that ran them, it didn't strike me as an especially complicated decision to have taken. Even then, a cursory mention of Bible John would provoke a reliable spike in eyeballs visiting their websites. Particularly when that mention came wrapped in a sensational new theory regarding a high-level and long-hushed-up conspiracy at the very top of Glasgow's notoriously clannish and insular police force. As theories go, the broad outline to it wasn't the most crankish, with police corruption and violence hardly novelties in Glasgow or elsewhere across the UK.

It continued to fascinate and amuse me that Harrison at least had the confidence trickster's good sense to lay down a vaguely solid structural foundation before adding the alarming rococo flourishes, like the ridiculously long and histrionic speeches delivered by Joe Beattie and Jeannie Williams and the enjoyably eggy cliché of the devilish uncaught killer living in a remote corner of the Highlands (of course, Harrison couldn't resist adding that 'he would have killed again'). In his own, more wilfully extreme way, Paul Harrison was simply continuing a long tradition laid down over the decades that had seen the creation of the Bible John myth. The tradition of increasingly turbo-charged and nonsensical theories that had only ever served to obscure the facts surrounding the three killings, which no one could apparently say with any certainty had even been committed by the same figure. The more I revisited his book, the more I grew to enjoy it in a way. Its very dishonesty and ridiculousness, carried to ever-more airless and disorientating heights. The strange book could be guiltily delighted in, as long as you chose to read it as what it was: an absurdist text. Harrison had lied and deceived to an almost obsessive degree. It was craven and retrospectively embarrassing, though not entirely devoid of a specific strain of gallows humour.

This couldn't be said for some of the more serious and straight-laced alternatives. From the very start, Bible John was a magnet for the most naked and unapologetic ambition. Joe Beattie's was perhaps the first example, even if no one could fault his earnestness, or has really managed or wanted to do so in the decades since. Though he was fatally stubborn and inflexible, few have ever doubted his deep personal connection to the case through his close affiliation with Jeannie Williams, his investigative muse. After he died in 2000 aged 82, the obituaries were as much devoted to Bible John as they were to the rest of Beattie's life and career. Whenever the case resurfaced in the press towards the end of his life, he had given a very different take to when the hysteria had been at its height in the late 1960s and early 1970s. When the McInnes news was dominating headlines in 1996, it was Beattie, now the wise elder statesman and monument to a very different time and place, who was quoted pouring cold water on the idea of a serial killer. But that hadn't quite been the case when he'd been running the investigation at the height of his power and authority. Though no one person could be blamed for the desperately dysfunctional and chaotic early inquiry, riven with incompetence and casual misogyny,

Beattie's dominant role could hardly be ignored. To many observers at the time, it felt like Mr Beattie might know only too well the opportunity that Bible John represented: the chance to transform himself into a legend.

Of all the sources that I'd come across, few were and have ended up being as useful as Alan Crow and Peter Samson's 1998 book *Bible John: Hunt for a Killer*. Its pages contain unparalleled detail on the weird, strained life of John McInnes and his brief afterlife as a *cause célèbre* in the Scottish press. It also reads like what it is: a book produced in a manic flush of activity after the first revelations had broken in late 1995. The chronology is fragmented, diving between the late 1960s and the then present day. The two journalists worked at the *Daily Record*'s sister publication, the *Sunday Mail*, and some of the book's content was taken from the initial news reports surrounding the exhumation that I'd read in my back-office perch in the *Daily Record* building. Like so many other journalists of the day, they'd hedged their bets that McInnes was Bible John. There are several sections that show the signs of hasty revision when it had become apparent McInnes probably wasn't the mythical serial killer at all.

When I spoke with Peter Samson over the phone in early May 2022, he told me he'd attended the exhumation, or rather 'observed from afar'. He and Crow were then 'locked in a room for several weeks to write the book'. Being staffers, there was no extra financial recompense attached to the project. It was just part and parcel of their everyday duties, he told me. The two were also working on a book about the 1996 Dunblane massacre, told through the lens of several of the victims' surviving families and loved ones. It was an intense time, he explained, with a fair hint of understatement.

Samson could still remember the morning of the McInnes exhumation fairly clearly. It was hard to forget really, he said. Then, as now, he wouldn't have exactly styled himself as a big fan of graveyards. Indeed, lurking around a cemetery isn't something he'd ever choose as a hobby. He's pretty sure that he can recall a bright sunny morning. Very bright, with a clear blue sky above that seemed to accentuate the enormity of what was happening in front of him. Something about the idea of an exhumation still catches him hard to this day. 'It must be the most enormous decision to make. Not just for the families of those that are left behind, but even for the authorities.' It must be, he explained, like opening Pandora's box. 'Seeing it was quite chilling, as there were [the] tents covering the grave. It was a big operation for what was essentially a six-by-two hole in the ground.' It was busy, he remembered, with police and white suits swarming everywhere. A silent hive of activity. He can still remember the quiet. If you were blind, he told me, you still wouldn't have heard a pin drop.

When I asked what it felt like when the inconclusive results of the DNA testing came through, Samson is clear enough. He couldn't even remember what day it was, though it was likely a Thursday or Friday when he heard the news. All the daily papers were going to have the story, but it had all been so long ago, it was hard to recall with any certainty. 'It was 1996 and that's twenty-six years ago. I struggle sometimes to remember what happened twenty-six minutes ago. It's like a different life when I look back on it, you know.' After our call, I'd emailed Alan Crow, as I wanted to hear his recollections of the time, and whether he'd continued to grip onto the Bible John story, while his co-author had clearly moved on. Despite sending several interview requests into the ether, I never did hear back from the former Deputy News Editor at the *Sunday Mail*.

A week before my call with Peter Samson, I'd taken the train from Glasgow Central to Lanark, a journey which takes an hour or so to drift pleasantly south through a succession of unglamorous outer suburbs and mid-sized satellite towns, from Cambuslang and Uddingston, to Motherwell, Wishaw and beyond.

On a bright Thursday evening in late April, it felt like good luck to catch the journey at its most picturesque.

The train was busy with the gentle hum of the daily commuter crowd whose numbers gradually thinned out as the train progressed along the line. On arrival, I took in the high street before doubling back on myself and arriving at Lanark Memorial Hall. *Dancing with the Devil* was already well into its run across Lanarkshire and beyond. The press coverage had been positive, if fairly light on detail. I'd been intrigued from the moment I'd seen a notice appear for it on the *Daily Record* website. It wasn't every day that came with the offer of a dramatic musical take on the killings.

> *1968. Glasgow's Dancehalls jiving & swinging to the sounds of the 60s. Gangs on street corners. The Clyde launching her last ships. Fashions taking on a new flare … but Glasgow loves to dance. Its dancefloors beating to a fab four and more … Remember The Palais, The Plaza, The Locarno?*
>
> *But the Barrowlands was rife. Rife with rhythm. Rife with rumour.*
>
> *Lurking in its smoky shadows was a serial killer. Murder on … and off the dancefloor.*

This press release promised a fresh reflection on the killings, stepping back into the fog of the past to recreate the grand old dancehalls of late 1960s Glasgow, with a few iconic musical numbers thrown in for good measure. Its director had been quoted in several pieces across the city's press, stressing that though he knew a Bible John musical sounded odd, it touched on a variety of wider themes, including the ubiquity of violence against women – just as live an issue in 2022 as it had been in 1969. He had been at primary school in Scotland during the early 1970s, when the name Bible John spoke to an ever-present bogeyman. And he had spoken to many others who had grown up in the era and collected their stories via social media. It was a tale ingrained in the Scottish mindset and not just the Glaswegian one, he explained. The musical wouldn't focus on a particular victim or her murder. And Bible John would be played by three different actors, to reflect the fact of the uncaught killer still squatting in the popular imagination. George Puttock had even given the production his blessing, as long as it didn't have anything negative to say about him or his family. Anything that kept Helen's name in the public eye could only be a good thing, he told the *Daily Record*.

The hall was almost packed out by the time the lights dimmed around seven. On arrival it had become clear that I was the youngest person in the theatre by at least fifteen years, a fact reinforced by the occasional quizzical look which bent my way from the rows of families and couples in the aisles around me. An elderly man winked and waved at the can of Diet Coke in my hand, a gesture I returned with a friendly smile, even if I didn't fully understand its meaning.

Three women soon appeared on stage in what was evidently supposed to replicate 1960s youth period dress: all short skirts and outrageously loud patterned blouses. After some vaguely bawdy patter, the scene cut to a dancehall at night where three men appeared from the darkness, snarling and prowling across the stage in overly tight tartan trousers: the three would-be Bible Johns searching for their next victim. The tone continued to jump in a way that felt increasingly alarming; from farce, to murder mystery, to heart-rending melodrama and back. Musical interludes came and went. It was clear enough from a cursory glance that the latter were what most of the audience had come for, as the fifty-something couple in front of me began to sway and cheer whenever one of the old hits came on. We were introduced to the hard-bitten and harder-drinking veteran detective running the subsequent murder inquiry, who shook and bawled and wept at the enormity of his burden (it had quickly been revealed he was also the father of the youngest of the three women we'd been introduced to, as well as a remorseful, if regular, wife beater).

A respectful hush had descended when a blown speaker and uncooperative backing track sabotaged one cast member's solo, as she stood frozen in place under the glare of the revolving silver disco ball overhead. The rest of the act passed in a blur. At the interval, I bought a glass of wine and stepped back to observe the people filing in and out of the theatre. I thought of how odd I must have looked and began to wonder why I'd made the journey and what I supposed this evening was or wasn't going to prove about the enduring fascination with Bible John. As the lights dimmed for the second half, there were two free seats where the enthusiastic couple in front of me had been sitting, which remained empty for the rest of the night.

THE DRIFTER

The first time I spoke with David Swindle was via Zoom in July 2021. It had been a fairly short and scrupulously polite call. We spoke about my plans for the book and exactly what it was I was hoping to achieve with it all. And indeed, why I was interested in the whole Bible John mythology at all. It seemed as if the answers struck the then 66-year-old as reasonable enough, as we ended our conversation by agreeing to set another date to meet in person, later in the year.

He had a right to caution when it came to Bible John and his own brittle connection to the murders. Before his 2011 retirement, David Swindle had spent thirty-four years with Strathclyde Police, most of them in CID, before eventually rising to Detective Superintendent. There wasn't much that he hadn't covered over a long and preternaturally successful career. Murder cases were common enough, as were rapes, robberies and human trafficking.

Indeed, he had likely dealt with hundreds of killings over the years, according to the biography on his own website, though Swindle seemed unusual in having studied for a degree in forensic medicine at Glasgow University, as well as a postgraduate qualification in Alcohol and Drug Studies. The same biography also speaks to his willingness to innovate and his role in 'developing crime investigation processes'.

It's the type of corporate jargon that can easily set one's blood to boiling point, though it had some justification in David Swindle's story. Most detectives go their entire career without a defining case, however senior they might climb. Years and decades pass, lived quietly in the slipstream of murk and violence, the everyday crush of misery and despair. It wasn't like that for Swindle. June 2007 had seen the then Head of Strathclyde Police Public Protection become the Senior Investigating Officer leading the inquiry following the Glasgow Airport terrorist attack, in which a burning jeep had been driven into the main terminal building. Gordon Brown had become Prime Minister three days earlier and the international media had quickly descended on the outskirts of Glasgow (no one was killed, save for one of the perpetrators, who later died from his burns in hospital).

Swindle's work on the inquiry – seen as a swift, decisive and high-profile success – earned significant media

attention and a glowing Chief Constable's Commenda-
tion. Swindle had provided 'drive and inspiration to
members of the ... team working under incredibly intense
difficult circumstances. Under the immense pressure of
worldwide media scrutiny, [he] ensured that the excellent
investigative reputation of the Force was upheld.'

That particular success wasn't why David Swindle
became one of the best-known police officers in the UK.
The same year had also witnessed one of the most
high-profile and sordid trials in recent Scottish legal history. In September 2006, a 23-year-old Polish student
called Angelika Kluk had been reported missing the week
before she was due to return home to Gdansk after a
working holiday in Glasgow. It wasn't Kluk's first visit to
Scotland; she had embarked on a couple of long trips
around the country in 2004 and 2005. By the end of her
second visit, she had become increasingly close to Father
Gerry Nugent, the long-standing and popular priest at
St Patrick's Church in Anderston, a large Victorian red-
brick pile dominated by the surrounding high rises and
motorway flyovers in Anderston, the working-class
neighbourhood on the western fringes of the city centre.
The area had fallen on hard times in the latter half of the
twentieth century, having been built into isolation during
the 1960s construction of the M8 motorway, which cut
the area off from the city centre proper.

The area's fortunes had gradually improved by the early to mid-2000s, though no one was accusing Anderston of hoarding any excess glamour. It worked well enough for Angelika Kluk. Her flat on Elliot Street was nearby and the church had rapidly become the central part of her life in the city. When her landlord asked her to leave the flat, Kluk had turned to Father Nugent for help. His offer was generous and immediate. There was a spare room in the chapel house, which he would be glad to give to her rent free for the duration of her time in Glasgow. When she returned in 2006, the same arrangement held. According to subsequent reports, the last trip was not such a glowing success. There had long been whispers surrounding Father Nugent's increasingly erratic behaviour and unignorable drinking problem that often drifted into blackouts and bouts of deep self-recrimination. Sometime during her 2006 visit, Kluk had become romantically involved with Martin Macaskill, a married 40-year-old businessman who ran a chauffeuring service. On Monday, 25 September 2006, Macaskill had sent Kluk the first in a series of increasingly anxious texts asking after her whereabouts after she had seemingly disappeared the night before.

St Patrick's Church was known for its open-door policy. Though increasingly drunken and unreliable, Father Nugent was still serious about many of his duties.

Around two months before Angelika Kluk's return, a wiry, grey-haired 60-year-old going by the name of Pat McLaughlin had shown up at the church, having been referred through the Loaves and Fishes homelessness charity, one of several active in the local community. The man was polite and well spoken, and keen to make himself useful if he was going to be offered help and shelter. McLaughlin was also a skilled handyman, who seemed to relish his new role completing any odd jobs that cropped up around St Patrick's. By the autumn of 2006 he had become a fixture at the church, though some of the long-time congregation thought it odd that the new arrival revealed so little about himself or his past. No one, however, thought it polite or necessary to press the attentive, enterprising figure who seemed so grateful to have been accepted into their community.

If this were a horror film, then the man's appearance would be told in the first scene. The sudden arrival of the mysterious, retiring figure invariably clad in a threadbare woollen jumper, soft voiced and unmistakably Glaswegian accented. The shy, almost grandfatherish figure who fitted straight into the texture of everyday life around the church. Always ready with the offer of a favour, or a few minutes of light and imprecise small talk. Lodged straight into the tight-knit inner-city faith community led by an increasingly erratic and out-of-control priest. Subsequent accounts stress how Pat McLaughlin looked good for 60. How strong and spry he was. How eager to please. They stress the intensity in his dark eyes, though of course they would. Anything to appropriately foreshadow what the visitor was about to become. What he was about to reveal.

It was later reported that Martin Macaskill had called Angelika Kluk's mobile over twenty-five times on Monday 25 September. By early evening, he'd decided to call Angelika's older sister, Aneta, who was also living in Glasgow. The two of them met at St Patrick's and made their way to Angelika's room, where most of her belongings sat untouched and apparently undisturbed. Handbag, wallet, laptop. Bank cards, passport and her return plane ticket to Gdansk. The only thing missing was her mobile phone. From there, panic rose to a new pitch. The police were phoned and arrived an hour or so later. They were greeted by Macaskill, Father Nugent and Aneta Kluk. Statements were given. Angelika was missing and no one had an idea where she might have gone. Everyone at the church supplied a statement, including the recent arrival, Pat McLaughlin. The day passed somehow, even with all of their worry and strain. They prayed and tried to sleep. There was a feeling, and nobody said it yet though perhaps everyone felt it, that something had gone very suddenly and very badly wrong. That something had changed.

On the Tuesday morning, not too long after first light, Pat McLaughlin gathered up his meagre possessions and left St Patrick's. The events of the day aren't known, though those of the night are. His phone had rung in the evening, a friend he had planned to meet in the city centre, though McLaughlin hadn't answered. It was late when he boarded the overnight coach to London at the St Andrew bus station in Edinburgh. His absence had already been noted back at the church. He hadn't turned up for work that morning and Father Nugent had immediately become concerned when his phone calls and texts hadn't been returned. He knew that McLaughlin suffered from a serious heart condition – the handyman had often complained about it in laborious detail – and worried for his health.

It wasn't long before the first reporters arrived at St Patrick's. The missing student was already becoming news. There was just something about the bare bones of the story as it was already beginning to take shape: a pronounced nothing-good quality. The police said that they wanted to speak with Pat McLaughlin, the disappeared handyman. But no one could trace him. There was a photograph of the man to go with the appeal, quickly disseminated to both the police and press. There was also quickly hardening talk that he was likely the last person to have seen Angelika before her vanishing. The missing girl was soon front-page news. Martin Macaskill publicly wept and pleaded for information. All he wanted in the world was for her to return safe and well. He loved her. Whatever it was or had been, it would be OK. His words were carried to the public by the *Herald* and the BBC. His wife, Anne, pledged to help and was seen around the local area, canvassing residents and handing out flyers. Despite the intensity of the coverage and the search, people were already beginning to speak about Angelika in the past tense as the days drifted on. Father Nugent offered a tribute to the girl 'who was taking life on and meeting it with such gusto and charm'. She had been so full of life, he said. She took part in everything and had loved Scotland, almost as if it were her other home. As each day went on, they were all praying for her very much.

Angelika Kluk's tarpaulin-wrapped body was discovered on Friday 29 September by a forensics officer who had opened a hatch on the floor next to the church's confessional box. Police had earlier discovered a loose table leg stained with her blood, as well as a pair of blood-soaked jeans in a bin on the church grounds. Kluk's hands had been bound and she had been tightly gagged. Her body was covered in a bin liner, which contained a blood-stained kitchen knife. She had been stabbed multiple times and her face was badly disfigured. She had been raped. A young female forensic scientist named Carol Weston descended into the hatch to recover the necessary evidence. The space was dark and cramped and bisected by a supporting wooden beam. Discussions had been carried out on exactly how to go about the job. Weston had been adamant. She had to examine the body in situ, rather than have it removed and taken to the police mortuary. There could be no chances taken. It had to be done right, and right meant descending into the hatch for three and a half hours, examining the body and collecting the various samples that would later be used at trial.

Pat McLaughlin was picked up at the National Hospital for Neurology and Neurosurgery in London, where he'd taken refuge complaining of serious chest pains. Though the frail sixty-something man who had checked himself in might have looked exactly like Pat McLaughlin, he had given the name James Kelly. Tests hadn't discovered the source of his pain and the attending doctor had been struck by his patient's lack of eye contact. A nurse at the hospital had recognized Kelly from the images now being disseminated far and wide, via TV and the national newspapers, under yet another name. Neither Pat McLaughlin nor James Kelly ever existed, but Peter Tobin did, as the news reports made clear. A male officer from the Met was involved in a moment of unlikely farce, when he arrived in the wanted man's room dressed in medical scrubs to identify the man whose face had by then already become synonymous with the missing student in Glasgow.

Peter Tobin was born in 1946 in Johnstone, a small Renfrewshire town around twenty-minutes' drive from the centre of Glasgow. The second youngest of eight siblings born to a council worker and housewife, the early signs weren't promising. According to his younger brother, Peter had always been wild. By the age of 7, he was placed in a reform school. By his teens, several later reports highlight his involvement in petty crime and theft. Some even mention an unsuccessful stint in the armed forces, though reports of him joining the French Foreign Legion have never been corroborated. In 1969, he married his first wife, 17-year-old Margaret Mountney. The relationship was marked by extreme violence. Tobin would keep Mountney prisoner at their flat in Shettleston, in Glasgow's East End. On one occasion, a downstairs neighbour had contacted police when blood began to drip through the ceiling from the Tobins' flat. It was only when he was arrested on burglary charges in Brighton a year later that Mountney managed to escape the marriage.

After serving three years of a five-year sentence, Tobin married his second wife in Brighton in 1973. Sylvia Jeffries managed to escape three years later, after a marriage that had produced a son and a daughter who had died almost immediately after being born. Jeffries was later to flee to a women's refuge and win a lifelong injunction against Tobin, preventing him from contacting or approaching her. Later, she recalled how her ex-husband had taken a job with the local water department early on in their marriage. He had seemed to enjoy it well enough. Part of the role involved intensive training on how to professionally dig trenches, a skill which seemed to coax something out of him. As if it was the most fascinating pastime in the world. The late 1970s and early 1980s remain something of a blank. Tobin was a drifter and never really settled anywhere for too long or too deeply, as he flitted between unglamorous towns and odd jobs. Later, there were people who remembered him, or thought they did, spread all over the country, with a particular emphasis on the south coast. The faintly charming and evasive figure. The quiet and self-contained neighbour. A peripheral blur, here for a moment and gone the next.

In 1986, the 40-year-old Tobin was introduced to 16-year-old Cathy Wilson at a biker bar in Brighton. She was young, naive and had grown up in a fractured, dysfunctional family on the south coast. The couple were living together within three weeks. Tobin had promised her work at a local cafe, though the job never materialized. It wasn't long before Wilson became pregnant. Their son, Daniel, was born a year later. In 1989, the couple were married and embarked on a move hundreds of miles north to Bathgate, a quiet, mid-sized town located midway in the sprawl between Edinburgh and Glasgow. The house on Robertson Avenue was a trap. Though the alternating bouts of charm, control and violence had begun long before the move, they quickly accelerated in Scotland. Cut off from any of her support networks, Wilson became further and further isolated. She eventually made her escape in April 1990, having secretly saved just enough money for a bus fare to London, with Daniel in tow. Word reached her that Tobin had attempted suicide after her flight. He had poisoned himself, the source told her, with amitriptyline, an antidepressant that could serve as a moderately potent tranquillizer when taken in enough quantity.

Wilson was to settle in Portsmouth, though her fresh start was tempered when Tobin performed one of his routine cross-country moves to Margate, the then faded and faintly seedy Kent seaside town. The move from Bathgate had been sudden and decisive. After he'd applied for a council house swap, it had been granted when a middle-aged couple living at the three-bedroom terraced house at 50 Irvine Drive had expressed interest in a move to Scotland. The threats began immediately after his return to England. He wanted access to Daniel and wouldn't stop until it was granted. By 1991, a regular-enough routine had been established where father and son would be reunited for the odd weekend together, spent at the house in Margate. It's said that the little boy particularly enjoyed playing in the cramped back garden. The next move arrived just as suddenly that same year, when Tobin rented a second-floor flat in a nondescript block in Havant, just a few miles from Portsmouth.

The events of 4 August 1994 have been the partial subject of several TV documentaries and dozens of newspaper articles in the decades since, memorialized as one of the crucial landmarks in Peter Tobin's squalid and repetitively brutal biography. The two 14-year-old girls had ended up at Tobin's door by accident. They had been calling on a neighbour, who was out. There is some discrepancy in the precise order of what happened next. Some accounts have the girls asking Tobin if they could wait in his flat a while, though others have it the other way around. Whatever the precise order of events, they entered, perhaps reassured by the sight of Tobin's 5-year-old son playing in the living room. They were given strong cider and vodka to drink. Tobin offered them some pills, he called them blues, and explained that he'd already taken three himself that day. The girls refused, though the alcohol soon took effect, with one of them passing out on the sofa. Tobin then appeared with a knife and told the still-conscious girl that he would kill her if she continued to scream. There was a struggle and Tobin was stabbed in the leg. Daniel wandered into the room and was immediately removed by his father. The girl was forced to down a cocktail of wine and pills, which eventually knocked her out.

The other girl woke around 6.25 a.m. the next morning, with a bloodied bandage around her wrists, a tie around her ankles and her friend lying unconscious next to her. After trying to wake her she fled and raised the alarm. The smell of gas was thick and unmistakable. After sexually assaulting the teenagers, Tobin had turned on the gas fire in the living room to full blast and left, having earlier phoned Cathy Wilson to come and pick up Daniel. In a mirroring of the same cringing self-abasement that later followed the murder of Angelika Kluk, he'd told his ex-partner that he was experiencing severe chest pains and urgently needed to go to hospital. From here, Peter Tobin vanished. Days after the teenagers' abduction in Havant, a man named Peter Wilson introduced himself to a day-tripping Christian group in Brighton. The Jesus Fellowship Group invited the charming and apparently destitute 47-year-old Scot back to their base at the King's House Centre in rural Warwickshire, where he soon offered to perform odd jobs around the place in exchange for shelter.

Suspicions grew over the man's lack of plausible back-story and evident discomfort when confronted with the most basic questions about his past. Peter Wilson was eventually asked to leave, which he acquiesced to with surprising meekness. A few days later, members of the group had tuned into the BBC's *Crimewatch* programme, which devoted a prominent section to Peter Tobin, the man they had briefly known as Peter Wilson. Tobin was arrested soon after in Brighton. At the subsequent trial, the presiding judge spoke of the potential lifelong impact on the two girls who had been viciously attacked. He offered to the court that 'it may well be [that] their prospects in life have been gravely and permanently impaired', before handing down a fourteen-year sentence. At the end of a brief news report on the trial, the *Independent* noted that the offences were apparently 'wholly out of character'.

On his release in May 2004, Tobin was put on the Sex Offenders' Register and moved to a flat in a Glasgow satellite town. Neighbours remembered a quiet elderly man who mostly kept to himself, save for a few afternoons at the odd communal barbeque. By October 2005 Tobin had vanished into the city proper, having been reported to police after threatening a 25-year-old woman with a knife. Efforts were made to trace him, though nothing came back. There was just under a year to go before Angelika Kluk was reported missing.

When the trial began at Edinburgh's High Court in March 2007, the tabloid press began to compete over the most lurid scoop. Father Nugent told a Sunday paper that he and Angelika had been lovers, a story that her sister instantly refuted in her own evidence to the court. The next day brought news of an affair with a guitarist in the church's band and a merciless public dissection of the priest's alcoholism and credulity. Tobin's defence eviscerated Nugent and the initially 'shambolic' missing person's search. Though Tobin strenuously denied murdering Kluk, it quickly became apparent that he had been the last person to see her alive. On 14 April, the *Daily Record*'s front page led with news of the jury being forced to watch a fifteen-minute video of Angelika Kluk's body under the church floorboards, which is described in as much detail as the paper could get away with.

After a six-week trial, Peter Tobin was found guilty of rape and murder on 4 May 2007. While handing down a life sentence, with a minimum twenty-one-year tariff, Judge Lord Menzies spoke directly to Tobin:

In the course of my time in the law I have seen many bad men and I have heard evidence about many

*terrible crimes which have been committed but I
have heard no case more tragic, more terrible than
this one. Any case of rape is serious. Any case of
murder is serious. But what you did to Angelika Kluk
was inhuman ... you are, in my view, an evil man.*

Angelika Kluk's sister shouted out her thanks to the
jurors as the verdict was read out. Later, the Kluk family
issued a statement detailing their relief at the sentence
and their thanks for the support from the Scottish public
right from the start of their terrible ordeal.

David Swindle had become a media fixture in the
run-up to the trial and has remained so long after its conclusion. It was his team that had gathered the forensic
evidence the conviction had eventually hung on (the evidence so carefully taken from Angelika Kluk's body, as
well as a blood-stained shirt found during Tobin's arrest)
and his team that were to lead the newly formed 'Operation Anagram', set up to trace the peripatetic Tobin's
movements over the previous forty years. Whispers had
begun almost as soon as Tobin had become the prime
suspect in the Angelika Kluk murder, rumours which
David Swindle was soon to outline to the press. The
ferocity of the attack had shocked detectives. It was rare,
vanishingly rare, for a 60-year-old man to have killed in
that way, or for the first time. It was possible that Tobin

had killed before, perhaps many times. The search scaled up fast and pulled together multiple different police forces. At its height, detectives across the country were tracing thousands of lines of inquiry, from the English south coast to the Scottish Central Belt. Bank accounts were uncovered and old addresses accumulated. It was thought that Tobin had driven and discarded up to 120 cars. Missing person files were reopened and pored through, for any connection to the thin, just about elderly man embarking on his life sentence.

Further searches of Tobin's previous homes in Margate and Bathgate in late 2007 revealed the remains of two more bodies. Vicky Hamilton and Dinah McNicol, two young women who had been reported missing in 1991, having last been seen in Bathgate and Hampshire respectively. There's no need to recount the particularities of their deaths. Both bodies were recovered from the back garden at 50 Irvine Drive, the narrow and unremarkable mid-terrace in Margate. The usual media circus descended, with former neighbours quizzed and pressed for a few scraps of detail about the dimly remembered man who had moved with such haste in the earlyish 1990s. Some thought they recalled a strange and occasionally sinister presence, though most confessed that they hadn't considered him anything other than a quiet and unremarkably private man.

Tobin was served with his third life sentence in 2009, while Operation Anagram was wrapped up three years later, having failed to officially uncover any other victims. It's difficult to conclusively state who first made the link between Tobin and Bible John, though Professor David Wilson features prominently in most accounts. No one has ever accused the Scottish academic and celebrity criminologist of being slow to scent an opportunity. Indeed, when it comes to media bylines and publicity, Wilson's storied twenty-five-year career is without contemporary rival in the UK. Much of his biography is well known, at least among the country's legion of true crime fans. It's often reported that he became the youngest prison governor in British history when he was appointed Assistant Governor at Wormwood Scrubs, fresh from his Cambridge PhD aged just 29 (the truth is slightly more complicated, though Wilson did work in the same role at a young offenders' institute during the same period). What isn't in doubt is Wilson's subsequent senior roles at HMP Grandon and HMP Woodhill, one of the most notorious prisons in the country.

The media appearances began in 1999 and have accumulated at a rapid rate ever since. If a serial killer documentary is being produced in the UK, then Wilson is a good bet to be involved, whether as talking head or presenter. From *Measuring Evil: Britain's Worst Killers*,

to *Killer Psychopaths* and *David Wilson's Crime Files*, the
list is dizzying long. To watch an episode of any of these
broadly interchangeable programmes is to understand the
core of Wilson's enduring appeal. Erudite, earnest and
totally respectful of the genre's conventions, he comes
across as every inch what we might expect of a criminal
profiler: a potent mixture of the tweedily academic and
the ruggedly hard bitten. He speaks fluently, weaving
facts with plausible, vaguely scientific theories. He doles
his insights out with precision and wraps up the obvious
with just enough dramatic panache to keep the viewer
hooked, or at least entertained. An equally prolific author,
he has written, or co-written, books on topics ranging
from a history of British serial killers to a plotted biography of 'The Suffolk Strangler' Steve Wright, who
murdered five sex workers in Ipswich over the course
of 2006.

In Wilson's telling, his Bible John eureka moment came
at Tobin's trial for the murder of Dinah McNicol. That's
how it's described in a 2010 article in the *Daily Record*,
timed to coincide with the release of Wilson's book *The
Lost British Serial Killer: Closing the Case on Peter Tobin
and Bible John*. The criminologist had been astonished to
see the links between Tobin and the quasi-mythical Barrowland killer stack up in real time. It was chilling to see
how they proliferated, he told the paper. Tobin was a

demented serial killer who had grown up in and around Glasgow. He had likely attended The Barrowland Ballroom and was known to be well spoken and attentive when he needed to be. There was a decent-enough likeness to the famous photofit and the killings had apparently ceased after Tobin had moved south. There was even a point when Wilson had wanted to stand up and shout 'Peter Tobin is Bible John!' Though there was no way of proving it beyond doubt, Wilson was confident enough that he'd stake his entire professional reputation on the fact.

The book is an awkward, discomforting thing. It mixes reporting and loose social history to paint a picture of Tobin and Bible John, before trying to tightly mesh the two together, with frequent bursts of novelistic imagination. Kluk's murder is reimagined in Penny Dreadful detail, along with Hamilton's and McNicol's abductions. There are chapters devoted to long and thinly sketched 'criminal profiles' of Tobin and Bible John, as well as the apparently unshakable similarities between the two, laid out in exhaustive, speculative detail. There are portions that feel rushed and incomplete. After 255 pages, the book ends with a simple declaration. 'Bible John? Case solved.'

For some, this has passed into canon law. The infamous killer finally caught in all but name after more

than half a century. There were, however, several problems with Wilson's hypothesis, particularly that Tobin's
first wife could provide a solid alibi for him for Jemima
MacDonald's murder, despite her loathing for the man.
The couple had been on their honeymoon, having been
married just ten days before. David Swindle was to publicly state that nothing in all the years of Operation
Anagram could link Tobin to the three historic murders,
a fact he reiterated to me during our first conversation.
Don't you think, he'd explained with a slightly exasperated smile, that we would have been all over it if there
had been anything at all substantial to go on? Though
he was sure that the extent of Tobin's crimes probably
remained unclear, he was absolutely categorical in his
denial that the sadist had anything to do with the Bible
John legend. The whole circus occasioned by Wilson's
book had been an irritant, he admitted. There was just so
much else to do and so many other leads to chase.

When I contacted David Wilson to see if he would be
interested in an interview to discuss his position on the
Bible John killings, the reply was brief and courteous. No,
he wasn't able to help, but he sincerely wished me luck
with the book. The initial automated response had listed
several alternative routes of contact. For media enquiries,
there was an agent. For urgent university work, a colleague could be reached first, while any information

about a murder case should be referred directly to the police. And no, he couldn't undertake private investigations.

The first time I met David Swindle in person was in early September 2021 in a high-ceilinged Glasgow bar not far from George Square. He'd arrived before me and had mentioned he'd be sitting at a table a slight remove from the main entrance. It was a warm, faintly hazy autumnal afternoon. We ordered coffees and almost immediately started back at Tobin and the origins of his association with Bible John. We spoke in detail about Operation Anagram and its dreadful revelations. Or at least that's what I took down in my notes, after Swindle had expressed that he'd rather I didn't electronically record our chat. Notes were fine, but my Dictaphone was not. There was a moment of high farce when I returned from the bathroom about halfway into our hour-and-a-half-long meeting. After smoothing down my coarse brown jacket, I was asked with evident sincerity (or at least a convincingly bland poker face) whether I was wearing a hidden wire.

No new ground was covered. We looped back and forward across the mid-to-late 2000s and arrived at the same conclusion I'd long already come to. Though Peter Tobin was a very real sadist and killer, he wasn't Bible John. Not for David Swindle, or almost anyone else who intimately knew the story in 2022. As we made our way to leave back into the afternoon sunshine, a middle-aged woman stopped Swindle at the bar to say she was sure she recognized him from somewhere. From the moment of his 2011 retirement, David Swindle has carved out a successful media career of his own, speaking regularly about Peter Tobin and his new ventures, including Victims Abroad, set up to aid the families of Brits who have died overseas. His face has almost become a fixture in the Scottish media, whether in print or on TV. He replied to the intrusion with a laugh and a modest wave of his arms. After a couple of beats, the woman's confusion melted into delight. Oh, from the telly, she'd beamed right back at the retired detective's embarrassed smile. On taking our leave, we walked down to Glasgow Central Station through the crowds of Buchanan Street revellers and parted at the entrance with a firm handshake.

There was about half an hour to wait for my train back to the Southside. Just enough time to reread my handwritten notes and cast my mind back to July 2018 and the last days of my first ever Bible John reporting trip. It had been a long week though there was one more stop I'd wanted to make, though I'm not really sure why now, just as I wasn't then.

It took about fifteen minutes to walk to Anderston from the city centre, give or take. It felt longer on account of having to navigate the concrete imposition of the M8 motorway that runs straight through what was once the area's heart. St Patrick's is a large and un-flashy red-brick building tucked in from the roar of the traffic, giving it a sense of quiet and repose. There was a man sitting outside enjoying a cup of tea in the midday sunshine. He told me with a smile that the church was closed. There wasn't much to say back. Turning around, it felt good to get back to all the life and noise.

THE DETECTIVE

July 2018 was unusually hot by Glaswegian standards. At least that's how it felt for the two weeks I was staying in an Ibis Budget located in a baleful retail park twenty minutes south-west of the city centre. The World Cup was on, though the pubs were quieter than they had been in London. Perhaps I shouldn't have been too surprised. Scotland had again failed to qualify, the latest of five consecutive failures spanning twenty years, while England were doing unexpectedly well – even beating Colombia in a penalty shootout, after a nervous and ill-tempered match. This wasn't, shockingly enough, cause for wild celebration in the centre of Glasgow.

The trip was a success, at least that's how it seems to me now at a few years' distance. I'd spent much of the time alone, in archives or occasionally meeting sources who could help explain different strands of the Bible John mythology. There were many miles of walking through the city, and many more hours spent in glum reading booths on the second floor of the Mitchell Library. Slowly, a picture had begun to emerge, or at least that's how it felt at the time. The places I'd only really read about that slowly revealed themselves and became familiar. Carmichael Lane, Bridgeton, the Barrowland itself.

Though most things had gone to plan, it seemed as if there would be a few disappointments. I'd particularly wanted to speak with Joe Jackson, the long-retired Murder Squad detective whose storied career had come to an end in the early 1990s. His name had cropped up repeatedly, right across the start of my research. He'd worked the Patricia Docker killing as a young detective and had a front-row seat for the birth of Bible John hysteria after Helen Puttock was found on 31 October 1969. He'd worked closely with Joe Beattie and had even served as one of the oft-derided 'Bible John Dancing Squad'.

I'd read his 2008 book, *Chasing Killers*, multiple times for its insights into the methods and history of policing in Glasgow. It nestles into the subgenre of true crime biographies that peaked in popularity during the late 2000s, full of breezily related hyper-violent anecdotes and mostly vivid period detail. The blurb tells you much of what you need to know. Credentials are laid out and authenticity is established, in the boldest terms. 'As a young cop',

Jackson was menaced by Arthur Thompson, notorious Glasgow kingpin of the 1960s and 1970s. As well as his part in the hunt for Bible John, Jackson also locked up 'more than his fair share' of 'sex beasts' and 'cracked the hardest homicide nut there is' (that is, a murder without a body).

Joe Jackson ('often called the real-life Taggart', the blurb also proclaims) didn't appear to be a shy man, at least from the impression of his literary output. Over the decades, he'd contributed to the odd documentary or article on Bible John, offering a few choice insights, usually delivered with an air of slightly inscrutable irony. But the 2010s had seen him drop out of the public eye, due to ill health.

I'd been passed his landline number by an acquaintance who worked as a reporter at a Scottish TV station. My first attempts were met by an answering machine. Three days before being due to travel home to London, I finally got through. Joe was reluctant. He told me that 'he'd spoken on this stuff so many times' that he wasn't sure what else there could be to say. After a minute or two, he'd relented, telling me to come down early the next morning.

The bus was quiet, with only a few elderly women for company on the top deck. After heading an hour south through increasingly sedate Glaswegian suburbia, I'd arrived at the start of a neat newbuild estate. Ten minutes later, I was greeted at the front door of a prim detached house by a man in his early seventies, wearing slightly owlish glasses accentuating a pair of shrewd, alert eyes. The next hour or two were spent sipping coffee in Joe Jackson's shaded back garden, our conversation falling straight into the world of Bible John, lurching across space and time from the late 1960s to the present day.

Our conversation has been edited for length and clarity.

Francisco Garcia: I don't want you to have to rehash all the things you've said before.
Joe Jackson: Anything you want to ask me, just ask.

FG: You were a young detective when you worked on the case, weren't you?
JJ: That's correct yeah. I was working in the Northside of Glasgow, in what was then called the North Division. Obviously, right, because it was in the north of the city. The nurse's murder happened in the Southside.

There were eight divisions in the city at the time. It generally happened that the call would go out to all of them when a murder came in. Two men, two detectives from each division. You'd go there and get given the menial tasks. Knocking doors, etc. So that's what happened. That was our job initially.

There was another side of the inquiry that should have been getting done. The divisional detectives should have been checking the types of people who are liable to commit these crimes [in the area]. This was a big problem with this particular crime. Really, what I'd have done if I was in charge of that – and I was in charge of many murders after that – was check the records. You always check your records. I have a feeling now that if they'd checked those records properly, this guy would have come up.

The situation was, the things we were doing, well it was merely checking and seeing if you could paint a picture with regards to what happened to this girl. It was obvious what happened. She said she'd gone to the Majestic but went to the Barrowland instead.

Those Thursdays, there was always a mix of people going without their spouses. Yes, it was called the Grab-a-Granny night. Initially, we were told by the people that interviewed her mum and dad that she'd been at the Majestic. There was the nutcase there who said he'd danced with her all night. You get a lot of these people, trying to be superstars. He got short shrift.

I was never involved in that side of the inquiry. There was the caravan near the locus. We came up one morning about two weeks in and the caravan was gone. We thought it was solved. But there'd just been the two murders over in Govan. Patricia Docker was left to the local division and I don't know how they approached it then.

FG: At that time, you can't have had an inkling about what would come next. It was a killing, among so many others.

JJ: No inkling. It was a killing. The girl was found lying up a lane. Her clothes were missing. I think she was killed in a car. She'd been near the lane, in a car, and he'd killed her, before driving away with the clothes. There was the river nearby. Some of her belongings were found there. There was talk at that time of the white car that had been seen in the area. I don't know about that, it was never brought up again in the inquiry.

That was as much as I had to do with it.

After that I went back to my division. Then there was the murder out in the East End. Jemima MacDonald. She was found in the close. The same carry-on. Strangled and raped. There was still no connection. Seriously, I don't know what the different divisions were doing. We're talking many years ago, the old-fashioned way of doing things. I don't know what was being done. I would love to have gone back and examined these two murders. I didn't get the chance to do that. Things roll on.

After a period working in the Flying Squad, I came back to the division. That was when the third murder took place, out in the Marine Division. It was running about three months before I was called in. That was Joe Beattie running the inquiry. I knew Joe. He was a senior detective to me, but we'd worked together before. He was a very strong character. You know, he was lucky, or that's what he thought. Seriously. He thought he was going to make his name. By that time, the killings had been linked.

[There is a brief pause here in the recording. An allowance for a tiny yapping dog darting over to sniff at the biscuit crumbs around my feet. After he's gently shooed away, we continue.]

I know you're in the press. My son's in the press, my daughter's friends too. But Beattie was giving them far too much. When I was eventually running inquiries, I was always careful. The press can be very, very helpful. Or they can be destructive. Right. You don't mind me saying that? You had to be very careful how you dealt with it. Joe had his picture taken outside the Barrowland and all that stuff. He quoted a thing to me one time, which [ended up] in the press. He said if he saw Bible John walking down the street, he'd know what pocket he had his change in.

That was the kind of character Joe was.

We were too focused on what he believed we should be doing. We should have been going step by step. Bible John should have been found. These inquiries should have been left to the individual divisions. We went to the dancing, we went to the dentists. There were so many people getting fired into the mix for all sorts of different reasons.

FG: So many that there were the cards handed out, specifying that people weren't Bible John?

JJ: I think there were about half a dozen people or something like that, given these cards. I'll tell you, there was a guy who ended up in a very senior [police] role, who was given one. He was just a young guy then, not at that level. Just a young guy, who liked going to the dancing. But he looked like ... he was pulled up so many times. He was a nice guy; I knew him personally.

The big problem was that Joe was pushing Jean, trying to get as much information as he could. They brought in the artist. Quite honestly, I think it was overdone. As a result of that, everyone got the wrong impression. They made him look special. The golden hair, the immaculate dress sense. You could see it yourself, when you went in to question people at the dancing. You'd say to a girl, 'Have you seen this man?' and she'd reply, 'I wish I had.' They made him such a good-looking guy.

It was an artist's impression and artists, as you know, will perhaps put their own slant on things. That was not the guy.

FG: Who was the guy then?
JJ: I think it was Peter Tobin. He had committed similar crimes before. How he slipped through the net at the time, I don't know. As soon as I saw Tobin, I thought that's as near as you were going to get. If you put him into the timeframe. Have you read what David Wilson said? If you look at that and the background to it. My own theory is that it was Tobin. I think it was Tobin. [But] I'm only an old cop speaking off the top of my head.

If you've killed three then, if you have any brains, you'd leave. And that's what he did.

Now I'm not being derogatory, I'm just being truthful. There were many times when uniforms would go to people's doors and not interview people the way they should have been interviewed. They wouldn't get the necessary information. When you're training as a detective, you know how important it is to get a full statement.

Everything was on paper then. You needed a good statement. If it didn't have enough information then you were lost. Things weren't computerized. There were all these kinds of problems going on. That should not have stopped good detectives looking at it and saying, 'OK, how do we solve this and how have we solved other crimes like it?'

FG: Why didn't that happen?

JJ: I don't know. I'm not blowing my own trumpet, but I did solve a lot of murders. You look at the background and say to yourself, where did that come from? With regards to Bible John, the guys who were running the earlier inquiries were happy when Joe Beattie took over because they could wash their hands of it. He's got it, we don't need it.

Joe tried to build a big picture. He thought this is mine, I want this. And it didn't work out for him. He was a good detective. He was a serious worker.

FG: It was a high-stakes gamble?

JJ: I know when you go into a murder inquiry, you look at every single thing you can. [But] everything was what Joe Beattie said. You had to go down that route. You could not deviate from his ideas.

He was talking to Jean a lot. Joe would finish his work at HQ and head back out to the Marine and sit there until three in the morning. He was always there. Always there working at it. He'd often have Jean with him, going through photographs. I had a feeling at that time, a few of us in CID did, that we'd been drafted into the inquiry so that she could have a look at us. We kind of resembled who she'd described as Bible John.

Unfortunately, I was one of the ugly ones, but I'm talking about some good-looking guys who matched the description. Joe used to bring them in so she could have a look at them. Everything was well meaning, but it was being run on one guy's say-so. You'd bring someone in and he'd take one look and say 'no'. Sometimes even with Jean sitting there, before she could even open her mouth.

That's how bad things got. Seriously. You didn't challenge Beattie. When he said that was it finished, that was it finished. But you just don't do that, you don't ignore any detective. Whatever they come back with, you listen.

I remember one inquiry I had. It was an old woman who had nearly been battered to death in the Gorbals. She was left lying in her room with a plastic bag over her head. She was taken to hospital and we began to check everything. I was a [Detective Inspector] at the time, with a wee squad working on it. There was a scientist from HQ, who produced these lights and started shining them in the door. He found a footprint, a very distinctive one, though you'd have never picked it up without oblique lighting.

We had this squad, with all these young guys too. One of them came to me and said there was a guy already locked up in Craigie Street whose print matched. He lived pretty much next to the old lady. It was him and his pal who had gone in. They got six years each. You listen to these young detectives because their minds are working. They're trying to prove themselves.

Beattie wouldn't do that; he wouldn't listen to anyone.

As a young cop, you want to [be involved]. I'd worked on several murders before [the Bible John killings] with some cracking detectives who really knew their stuff. Who knew every angle. There was one time where I'd asked to go indoors, during a murder inquiry in Easter-house. Learning while I was working, about how it should be done.

When you're running a murder inquiry, everything needs to be joined up. I feel with Bible John, these things were not done.

[Another brief silence, terminated by my audible, anxious sip of the last dregs of coffee in my mug. Joe laughs.]

JJ: Sorry, you've just had to listen to an old man talk a load of shite here.

HYPERVIGILANCE

I'm not sure who saw who first at Lockerbie Station on a humid, overcast morning in late August 2022. My train from Glasgow had pulled in a little early, so I'd taken a couple of aimless loops of the station, past a row of low grey houses and deathly quiet pubs. Around a quarter past midday, a black Audi had pulled round the corner at the agreed-on time. Having clambered into the passenger seat and shaken hands with the driver, a diminutive blonde woman in her mid-seventies, we quickly spun round and climbed out of the town-centre traffic onto Carlisle Road. After a ten-minute drive we'd arrived at Somerton House Hotel, a heavy slab of Victorian sandstone with a white conservatory protruding sharply from its side. I noticed that the car park was almost empty as we made our way inside through a doorway flanked with hanging baskets and two extravagantly sculpted sandstone lions.

Inside was as quiet as I'd expected. Any traces of midday August sun had vanished by the time we made our way through the main bar, our footsteps muffled by the plush red carpet underfoot. My companion chose the table, a four-seater not too far from a window that overlooked the car park and the rolling dark green hills in the distance. A few tables down sat a pair of genteel-looking elderly women, chatting conspiratorially over a pot of tea. We ordered coffees and I thought about instigating some gentle small talk with my companion, though it had rapidly become clear that this wasn't really Pauline Badger's style. After I'd set my Dictaphone down, she'd rifled through her handbag for her glasses. Though the performance took less than a minute, it was time well spent. She managed to tell me that she'd been at the police station that morning to give evidence on an unspecified crime and that I was a lot younger than she'd been expecting. It was her nature, it followed, to be precise, she continued in her clipped Mancunian accent. To do things in a very set and streamlined order. With the first thing following into the next, as logic should dictate. She had spoken to someone extremely senior in the military recently, who had mentioned their shared hypervigilance. Did I know what that meant? No, I wasn't sure. It meant existing in a state of constantly heightened alertness. Of walking into a room and scanning it at imperceptible speed for any danger, real or perceived. In her earlier years, it was a trait – or was it a gift – mainly focused on trying to identify IRA bombs before they were detonated.

That's why she'd managed to recognize Bible John after all these years. It was as close as that, she told me, pointing an arm at the dining room where two middle-aged patrons slurped at their soups with bowed heads. They'd been less than ten feet apart. So close and so long ago; she hadn't even realized until she'd seen the picture on the television. Anyway, she said after her arm had returned from the recesses of her handbag, still minus her reading glasses. What was it you came all this way to interview me for?

I'd come across Pauline Badger's story at the end of January 2022. It wasn't long after a two-part Bible John documentary had aired on the BBC, followed by a slow drip of news stories and follow-up pieces, mostly rehashing the story for the local news in Glasgow and its immediate surrounds. The programme was well made, though scant of much new information. It had ended with a dramatic flourish, with a brand-new artist's impression that had been laboriously composed to show what the killer might look like over fifty years on. The resulting image was of a severe and heavily lined face, below thin, dirty-blond hair. On 25 January I'd seen an intriguing piece published in the *Scottish Sun*, headlined

Spitting Image – I'm convinced I met Bible John: I didn't make the link until I saw new photofit of serial killer. It explains how a 74-year-old Dumfriesshire resident had been transfixed on watching the programme, with its new and updated photofit of the handsome, mocking figure who'd murdered three women in late 1960s' Glasgow. Pauline Badger had immediately contacted the authorities. There was no way she could be any surer. She'd seen that face, the pale smiling figure with the crooked teeth. The encounter had occurred when Badger worked as a stewardess at RAF Halton, one of the largest bases in the country, hundreds of miles south in Buckinghamshire. It was as if she had a mental map of him walking and talking with those strange front teeth.

The man was a technician who spoke as if he had a cigarette lodged in his mouth, even when he didn't. Badger repeated this for my benefit when we settled down after our coffees had arrived. In response, I'd tried to explain succinctly what it was I'd been working on. My well-rehearsed speech on how I wasn't looking to solve the case, nor did I hold the unshakable conviction that this might even be possible at all. How I was more interested in the history of the story and its reverberations down the decades, as well as the vivid, outsized place it still held in the minds of so many Glaswegians, and indeed so many people further afield, I hastened to add.

She'd taken this in quietly before fixing me with a tight, slightly quizzical smile.

In the preceding weeks, we'd exchanged messages over WhatsApp after I'd tracked down her LinkedIn profile, a platform where Badger is an active and enthusiastic participant. Her profile listed a dazzling array of qualifications and professional achievements. Over the years, she had worked as an ethnographer, historical researcher and unspecified freelance consultant on innumerable crime scenes and legal cases across the UK. According to her own sprawling biography on the site, she remained proud of her time in the RAF, having served between 1966 and 1969 as a stewardess at RAF Halton, while undergoing training at Spitalgate and Hereford. She'd worked in the Officers' Mess and as a VIP stewardess and served the Royal Family along with various other 'dignitaries on those functions and bases'. The following years saw her climb to Senior Aircraftswoman before moving to Singapore with her husband, a committed RAF man. The decades after that are left blank up until 1997, when she began an undergraduate science degree at the Open University. After that came a master's in Medical and Behavioural Sciences and, in her words, a decade and more of collaborating with police forces across the country and beyond, assisting them as they try to crack the most fiendishly difficult cases.

Though I'd already brushed up on her garlanded career and manifold successes, Badger was quite happy to fill me in again, before I could get a question in. Language mattered, she told me. Indeed, 'Bible John is a creation of language. I put this on purposefully,' she said, gesturing to a pearl crucifix around her neck. 'It's like a taunt to Bible John. That's where I am. I really think things through.' Just for the sake of the recording, I wondered if we could start with some more of her own biography. I wanted to know how a Lancastrian woman living in the Scottish Borders came to be so invested in such a resolutely Glaswegian story. In short, I wanted to know a little bit more about her before we arrived at Bible John and any of her more specific thoughts on his identity. It wouldn't be that simple. Instead, she began by outlining a few of her own choicest ethnographic theories (the study and observation, she wanted to remind me, of people in their natural environment). In Badger's telling, it meant separating 'normal rubbish' from 'unique rubbish'. Though I wasn't quite sure I understood, she'd pressed on. 'Everyone wants to fit Peter Tobin into it. But Bible John was selective. [They] haven't realized because they haven't immersed themselves [in the case].'

Pauline Badger was born in 1947 to a large Irish Catholic family in Manchester. Her early life in Salford was tough, though she didn't want to use the word poverty. She'd spent her teens and early adulthood around a range of colourful villains in the area and had been an avid attendee at a dancehall run by Jimmy Savile. That was about all she wanted to tell me about her youth, though she was happy to explain in detail how things took a darker turn when she'd met Ian Brady when she was 15, while working in a local department store. She had a lot to say about this, as well as him and Myra Hindley and the children killed on Saddleworth Moor. In fact, Badger had a lot to say about murder in general. Ideas and theories came freely, even before our coffees arrived. In her mind, Bible John was a bloodthirsty moralist. That was the only thing that made any sense. 'It wasn't for sex. It was to change these young women's lives around. He was trying to convert them. That's my view. These women were getting passed over in the nightclubs. Why were they going out with children? And why did they bring a man back when they had children?'

When I politely ventured that it was common knowledge that both Patricia Docker and Jemima MacDonald were estranged from their husbands, Badger was undeterred. 'Estranged is an academic word.' She wanted to stress that her interest in the case didn't stem from anything as lowbrow as a prurient obsession with true crime, but from sober, rigorous academic analysis. A few weeks earlier she'd sent me a lengthy voice message, when I'd

initially explained exactly why I wanted to meet and
speak with her face to face. About how I was particularly
interested in people who were still so avidly fascinated in
the myth of Bible John, half a century on from the very
real killings it represented. She had let me know that this
had been an extremely poor choice of words. She wasn't
a 'fascinated' armchair detective. No, she was interested
as a witness.

Amid the overlapping streams of information and
minute detail, we'd eventually got on to the topic of Rita
Ellis, a 19-year-old servicewoman who was murdered at
RAF Halton on 11 November 1967. It was what it
remains today: a sad, savage tale without anything in the
way of resolution. On the night of her death, Ellis had
been asked to babysit for one of the most senior figures at
the base, a Wing Commander named Roy Watson. First,
she had been escorted to the front of her accommodation
block by a young RAF apprentice and his girlfriend, who
left Ellis at 7.25 p.m. to head off on their date night.
When Watson arrived to collect Ellis, she was gone. He'd
waited for a quarter of an hour before leaving to get his
wife, who would be allowed to enter the women-only
block, under RAF rules. But Ellis was nowhere to be seen
inside. Another car had pulled up before Watson's white
sedan, which Ellis apparently willingly entered. Later,
investigators believed that she likely took the figure to be

Watson, who she hadn't met in person. The last sighting of her alive was at 8 p.m. It was a Saturday night and the base was even busier than usual due to a disco and bingo night open to service people and local civilians alike. In the commotion, no one gave much attention to the car drifting slowly across the base. Ellis's body was found by a dog walker the next morning by a piece of woodland on the western fringes of the camp. The killer had made a cursory effort to cover her body under some foliage. She had been beaten and strangled with her own underwear, while the postmortem brought up evidence of sexual assault.

The case was immediately taken up by Scotland Yard in London. A local scrap dealer was questioned and released when his blood didn't fit against a sample recovered from the murder scene in the woods. Something strange happened at the inquest, straight out of the most hackneyed crime drama. The coroner ventured that he was almost certain that the killer would 'strike again'. In the following months, two teenagers were attacked nearby, in the same corner of rural Buckinghamshire. Then a student nurse from Tring was attacked three miles from where Rita Ellis had been killed. The woman had been raped and beaten with a 'blunt instrument'. Despite her injuries, she survived to give a description of her assailant. The man was aged between 25 and 35, with a long face and puffy eyes. Though there were no definitive links between the crimes, speculation mounted that they were all the work of the same shadowy figure. Before too long, however, the investigation had burned down to nothing. No leads, no suspects and nothing approaching an ending. The crimes never really drifted into the wider public imagination, at least until 2007 when Thames Valley Police publicized a new 'cold case review' on the fortieth anniversary of Ellis's death.

Though that failed to yield any answers, another appeal was launched a decade later, marked by a few headlines centred on a new DNA sample that was to be tested against the national database. Ellis's family were gently warned not to expect too much, even if a suspect was identified. It wasn't certain that the killer, whoever he might have been, would even be alive to face a trial after so much time had passed. In 2021, the case received further prominence in a Channel 4 documentary presented by Professor David Wilson and actress Emilia Fox (best known as the lead in the kitschy long-running BBC crime drama *Silent Witness*). *In The Footsteps of Killers* sees Wilson operating at his theatrically supercharged peak. Having bestowed several glittering insights (including that Rita may have known her killer) he reveals that critical evidence related to the case has been sealed away in the National Archives until 2070, marked as classified 'for reasons of national security'.

After I'd ordered a second coffee, Badger told me that she'd known Ellis. Not well, though the two were on friendly terms and had overlapped during their time at RAF Halton. She was the shy, plain girl on the periphery of social life on the base and that had never been Badger's role. But yes, she'd definitely known the victim. Ellis had even borrowed money from her. Not much, but enough that it was still clearly a vivid recollection over fifty years later. 'I couldn't work out why she was always broke; she didn't really drink or anything like that.' Not long before her murder, she had approached Badger one afternoon and explained that she thought she was going to be attacked. And, of course, Badger had reported this to Thames Valley Police when she'd seen the case publicized many years later.

The Bible John killings had only begun a year later, and Badger was convinced there had to be a connection. Everything she'd read about the Glaswegian story seemed to bear exactly the same hallmarks as Rita Ellis's murder. It seemed odd, didn't I agree? The same man had to be responsible. The man she'd known from RAF Halton. Between Ellis's killing and Patricia Docker's murder, Badger's division was shipped abroad, though they would have been on leave throughout the dates separating the killings. It matched up perfectly. Did it, I wondered? It matched, I was assured. The ID papers that Bible John had allegedly flashed to Helen Puttock could have been an RAF-issued railway pass, which could have only been issued at the time. It would have been a pink slip of paper, which would have been appealing to a forces wife. 'He probably said to her I'm Sergeant (or Officer) Such-and-Such.'

Though I wasn't sure I followed, there was another set of questions I wanted to ask, as tactfully as possible. Badger hadn't come across Bible John until the BBC documentary aired in early 2022. It wasn't a name that meant anything to her before that, she admitted to me. I wanted her to describe that moment of recognition. What did it feel like? And how quickly had she felt certain that she'd met the figure captured in the new drawing? There was a slightly frosty edge to the first part of her reply. 'It didn't really bother me, it's just another Jack the Ripper. I'm not a fantasist or armchair detective,' she repeated. 'I thought, well, this documentary is on, I'll watch it. I know people think it was Peter Tobin, but I don't think it was him.' It was, she explained again, something she knew from the second she'd seen the photofit. 'I'd seen him before [and it was] like I'd seen him again. More than seen. I felt him.' I decided to change tack. What, if as many agreed, the famous portrait wasn't quite as accurate as it had once been billed? 'You've got to think about proximity. She was sitting next to him in the taxi. How many people do you sit next to that closely?'

The police had taken Badger's report very seriously. Yes, she had pestered them until they'd taken a statement. The piece in the *Scottish Sun* had borne this out, with a polite generic statement at the bottom of the article detailing how they welcomed all new leads and were still refusing to rule anything out regarding Bible John. Where did this leave her theory then, and were there any other interested parties she'd spoken with about the case? 'I haven't got a theory about Bible John. I don't do theories', was the swift response, though she was planning to attend the upcoming Glasgow Crime Convention in early September.

Pauline Badger wasn't the only person to report a fresh Bible John sighting to the police in the aftermath of the BBC documentary. It was a tale as old as the killings themselves, that had occurred throughout the decades. There would be a spark of some kind – a book, a newspaper feature, a documentary. An accusation that made the tabloids. The old photofits and artists' impressions would be wheeled out to spark something in a murder-hungry public. Anything to keep the legend alive. Then the game would begin afresh, with a steady stream of information sent to police and reporters alike. The *Daily Record*'s crime reporter Jane Hamilton had even written a piece on the burst of new activity and accusations. It mentioned a lab technician and a fairground worker, two local Glaswegian oddballs who had lived in the city during the late 1960s. They had come from exceptionally religious backgrounds or had been fond of quoting scripture. The same old story, repackaged and resuscitated until the news cycle moved on and relegated Bible John back to the shadows.

My conversation with Pauline Badger in Lockerbie had soon begun to skip across multiple different killings and theories, a densely knotted spider's web of detail and counter-detail. I sat and listened, interjecting where and when it seemed appropriate. It seemed as if she enjoyed having someone to speak with about the mass of violence and its enduring mysteries (most of her community gathered online, though she did have a team of like-minded collaborators she occasionally met in the flesh), and I was happy enough to let it all wash over me. We lost sight of Bible John and returned to the Yorkshire Moors, before striding back down to RAF Halton and beyond. An hour passed, then two before my head began to spin. At last, I made my excuses and said I'd better start thinking of getting back to the train station and making my way back to Glasgow, as a bout of industrial action had crashed an already spotty timetable into severe unreliability. That was fine, she said. There were other things she needed to do with her day, but she'd drop me off before running her errands and returning home to her house – the biggest in the complex, she assured me – where she lived alone and had done so for quite some time.

THE REPORTER II

By the late 2010s, if you read about Bible John in the *Daily Record* then you'd likely read a Jane Hamilton byline. The deeply experienced crime reporter had covered it all, including every new lead or fresh false alarm that periodically cropped up, as it did after the BBC's 2022 documentary aired.

I'd spoken with Jane a few times over the course of my reporting, and she was always unfailingly helpful and generous with her time and insights. When we spoke at length for the second time in the early autumn of 2022, she had just left the *Daily Record* after a long association with the tabloid. She had been covering crime for a long time, she told me with a laugh. And if she wasn't done with it exactly, then it was certainly high time for a break. I'd wanted to talk with Jane as it seemed important to document the ongoing link between the *Record* and Bible John – a knotty and often-difficult relationship by now well over half a century long. Aside from a couple of other honourable exceptions, it was hard to find another working journalist with the same depth of knowledge and self-awareness regarding the killings.

Hamilton had long been close to George Puttock and was planning to visit him later in the year, being mindful of his ill health. They had first met many years before during a temporary lull in interest around the murders. It had been tough for Puttock to understand why no one seemed to be interested in his wife's killing any more, and why her name had been allowed to fade from the public eye. From those beginnings, Hamilton and Puttock had spoken often and at length, collaborating for many different pieces until Hamilton's decision to leave the paper.

It would be a mistake to think Bible John represented Jane Hamilton's entire career, or that it was an obsession, or anything like that. Though it wasn't to be denied that she had devoted a great deal of her working life and energy to the story. There was always something new to report, whatever it did or didn't add to the already vast body of Bible John literature. Always something that cropped up to bring the old story back to life and a new readership.

Our conversation has been edited for length and clarity.

Francisco Garcia: How did you end up as a crime reporter?

Jane Hamilton: Strangely enough, it was by default. I was actually a transport reporter at the *Edinburgh Evening News*. You know, covering trains, planes and automobiles. The crime reporter before me had left and they didn't have anybody.

I was covering the bus wars at the time. Edinburgh was engaged in this massive, almost OCG [organized crime group] style bus war between these two companies and it was getting really heated between them. We were strapped [for people] one day and this drug story had broken. The news editor said, 'Jane, I know this isn't your speciality but can you just do it?' So I did.

About three days later I got what ended up being the Scoop of the Year. I got wind from a contact [who] told me that Edinburgh was getting rid of its tolerance zone for sex workers. Well, Leith more specifically. If you call Leith part of Edinburgh, you can get your head chopped off. The Port of Leith was very well known for its street prostitution. The police had traditionally turned a blind eye to it for decades. I'm talking about many, many decades, probably back to the Forties, Fifties and Sixties.

The women were given a free rein as long as they didn't annoy the local residents. That went for the kerb crawlers too, who were exempt from prosecution. Edinburgh was quite forward thinking and they were trying to follow the Dutch model for the policing of sex workers. I'd got a tip-off that they were scrapping it and planning to criminalize the women. Not the kerb crawlers. The women. This was the early 2000s and [it was thought] that big strides had been made. Edinburgh had come through the AIDS crisis and there had been a lot of work going on with the women, trying to ensure their safety.

Anyway, that was the story. It went national and worldwide. And I thought, well, I quite like this sort of world, I'm bored with buses. So I started to do more and more crime. I did an Unsolved Murder series, and the rest is, as they say, history.

FG: When did you start at the *Record*?
JH: Eight years ago, though that was my second stint. I was with the *Sunday Mail* from 2004 to 2008. I was at the *Sun* after that. Then freelance. And the *Record* managed to entice me back in 2014. I stayed another eight years. I've been everywhere.

FG: Always in Scotland?
JH: Yeah, I never had any desire to go to London, or anywhere else. I think crime is more ten-a-penny in London. Up here, crime is always quite an important subject in a way it isn't down south unless it's something like Soham

or Sarah Everard. Crime sells up here. That's why it's a focus for a lot of the papers up here. Crime is [often] better on the front page than politics.

It goes through phases of popularity. Since Netflix, the true crime world has exploded and there's a lot more interest in it. I've been plying my trade for twenty-three years and the last four or five have seen a massive change in attitudes. The public wants to hoover it all up. They just want to hoover up true crime.

FG: Was Bible John something you'd been aware of for a long time, or did that only come later when you became a crime reporter?
JH: I was vaguely aware of it. There's a weird dynamic in Scotland. The east and west don't really pay much attention to each other. Edinburgh had its fair share of murders. The city has its own dark stories to tell but you were vaguely aware of these big stories from further afield.

I know it's probably not what people want to hear, but we are a very parochial nation. We're closeted in our own areas. So I was aware of Bible John, of course I was. It would come on the news now and again, or you'd pick up a paper and someone would be doing something on it. But it didn't really start to fascinate me until I started at the *Sunday Mail*.

I'd gone down to the archives one day and came across all the Bible John files that we used to have. I just became fascinated by it and asked my boss if I could investigate it. And I've done nothing but investigate it since, what, 2003?

FG: That's why I enjoy talking to people who have such a long history with the story. Your thinking on it must have changed so much over the years?
JH: Yeah. It probably wouldn't have been such a massive part of my career if it hadn't been for Peter Tobin.

I was the first journalist to break his story and to interview his wife and son. I interviewed all three of his wives actually and was very much involved in the Angelika Kluk story. I went over to Poland to meet her family and was there the day her body was found in the church. Tobin became entwined with Bible John. And back in those early years there was always this thing in the back of my head. Maybe he is? Or maybe he was responsible for one of them?

But then you dig into Tobin and realize that he couldn't have been responsible for any of them. The evidence just isn't there to put him at the scene of any of the Glasgow murders. I'm no Tobin cheerleader. I absolutely despise the man. But he isn't and wasn't Bible John. I was so involved with both cases and they were [so heavily linked] ... well everybody thought it was him. I've kind of been fighting against that for all of these years as well.

You know, the Bible John story maybe took a back seat. But the narratives are so close, it was impossible to do one without the other. And then I became friendly with George Puttock. No one had written anything about it for a long time, until I did. And no one had approached George for a number of years. He thought everyone had forgotten about [his wife], until I started writing pieces about it.

Until I started dredging it all up again. You always have that fear, certainly when you're coming at something new that hasn't been in the public eye for a long time. That you're just dredging up pain for these families. But you realize that bringing these so-called 'cold cases' back with the best of intentions, well it can make the family feel better. It makes them feel like their relative hasn't been forgotten.

There's the chance that someone might come forward with information. Like the Mary McLaughlin murder.* The forensic scientist saw my story in the paper, when it hadn't been covered for about twenty-odd years. I'd come

---

* Mary McLaughlin was strangled in Glasgow in 1984. In December 2019 Graham McGill was arrested following a cold case review and found guilty of her murder in 2021.

across it doing [the] Unsolved Murder series, because that's obviously my speciality. I wrote a big story with her daughter and these things do make a difference. You don't know who's talking to who about it. And thirty-five years later they got the guy.

That's the way I approach these stories. I'm not doing it just to have a byline, or just to have a story in the paper. I do it with the best of intentions in the hope that these unsolved murders can be solved, or that we can at least get some answers for these families who spend years, who think everyone has forgotten about their relative.

FG: And that's the reality of it all. There were these victims and these families who were devastated.

JH: It's the women that need to be the centre of this story. I've been guilty of it myself. The story becomes about the killer. I've done it with Peter Tobin. The story becomes about him and the victims do get pushed to the side. They get pushed aside when they should be at the front of it from the very beginning.

A lot of what George and I have done over the past ten years is remind people that three women were murdered. It's been challenging as the other families never wanted anything to do with it, so it became centred around Helen because I can't speak for the other two families.

FG: These families were all different and approached their grief differently.

JH: There was another story I did, from the Sixties as well actually. The murder of a woman who nobody had ever written about, apart from briefly at the time. I approached her then-elderly son and told him I'd like to do a story about his mum, and did he mind? He and his daughter were so lovely. They welcomed me into their home and told me everything. I was able to investigate the murder and the upshot was that the police eventually named a suspect.

Almost fifty years had gone past and they'd never had a name. It had plagued him his whole life. He was 72 and he said that no one had ever cared about what happened to his mum. The police couldn't get any evidence and as so often with these things, it died a death, for want of a better phrase. There hadn't even been a cold case review.

That was my motive for writing about it. I knew there hadn't been a review and I wanted to get it out there. People criticize when we bring up cold cases. I hate the term but it's difficult to call them anything else. We bring up these unsolved murders, but if I can't bring anything new to the table then I'm not doing it.

THE CONVENTION

The date of 10 September 2022 had been marked in my diary for quite some time before I'd made my way up to Scotland the month before, for yet another Bible John reporting trip. Before leaving home, I'd vowed that this would be different from the ones that had gone before. No more living alone in whichever hotel or Airbnb presented itself. Instead, I'd decided to lodge with my old friend Sonia in her flat's temporary spare room, for the chance of some companionship, as well as some necessary perspective from someone who wasn't spending their waking life with a half-mythical serial killer.

The 9.07 train from Euston to Glasgow had been cancelled and the replacement severely delayed. Tempers soon rose and passive aggression flourished in the stuffy, overcrowded carriage. Hours passed before I finally arrived in Glasgow via Edinburgh Waverley, where I caught a taxi down to Mount Florida, a solid little chunk of suburban Southside. I'd quickly unpacked and made sure to stow the tattier or more alarming crime paperbacks underneath the tasteful literary fiction I'd also made sure to bring.

I'd seen the upcoming Glasgow Crime Convention advertised online earlier in the summer, before Pauline Badger had mentioned it over WhatsApp. An American invention, it was the first of its kind to be hosted in the city, following a few years of thriving London events. The premise was simple enough, whether in Las Vegas or the towering Hilton Hotel yards from the M8 motorway which cleaved through the centre of Glasgow. 'True Crime', as the official website puts it in unmistakably giddy advertising speak, 'is so much more than murder recreations and dramatic courtroom showdowns.' In fact, it would be a profound mistake to ignore the complexity and richness of a genre stuffed with 'real-life stories of triumph and tragedy; heartbreak and heroism'. There would always be something for everyone. Fun for the entire family, or at least for those interested 'in the criminal mind ... the criminal act [and] the criminal justice system leaping into action'. It was about nothing less than science, art, psychology and history. Perhaps more than anything it was, as the mission statement promised, a reflection on the way we live now.

Each event could offer a diet of talks from the very best podcasters and documentary makers, as well as the insights doled out from a revolving cast of detectives and forensic experts. It was all about creating the perfect balance, between the educational and the experiential, to curate a programme that had more than its fair share of 'hands-on learning' and fun centred on meeting the great and the good of the true crime community. But that wasn't everything. There was hardly a day that went by when the team at the American Crime Con HQ didn't soberly contemplate the victims. Of course, everything they did was grounded in respect for the families left behind, as well as the law enforcement officials who spent their time chasing the terrible killers and sadists who formed the basis of the talks and panel discussions. The Glasgow event promised to uphold these deep-set values, as I'd been informed over the phone by one of its organizers, Susie Fraser, an experienced public relations expert and writer, who had spent much of her distinguished career split between her home city and London.

Tickets to Glasgow Crime Con came in at £230 a head, though Fraser was happy to allocate me a press pass on good faith that I wouldn't trash the event. It was all about the victims, she'd repeated over the phone. She'd also explained that she knew the Bible John saga intimately, having grown up in a journalistic family who'd been around the city throughout the peak of its initial hysteria.

The entrance lobby was already crowded by the time I'd arrived at the Hilton around 10.30 a.m., jostling with a mixture of arriving crime fans as well as the outrageously well-sculpted figures I took to be the athletes arriving for the Davis Cup tennis matches that were scheduled for the coming days, according to the signs dotted around the ground floor.

The convention had taken over the spacious conference rooms on the hotel's third floor and it was clear enough that the programme had already hit its stride by the time I picked up my pass and made some introductory small talk with the solicitous Fraser and some of the other organizers at the stall by the entrance, which offered a range of Crime Con branded merchandise for sale (£14 would get you a water bottle, though a bookmark could be purchased for a third of the price). I explained that I was happy to just observe for a while, though I'd perhaps be keen to speak with some of their guests later on in the day.

The attendees were more diverse than I had expected, but what exactly was it that I'd had in mind? The reality was a tangle of smiling middle-aged couples, who walked by hand in hand through the foyer, stopping only to dreamily skim the blurbs of the books piled onto stalls manned by eager young booksellers. A number of lone women around the same age loitered slightly awkwardly by themselves, turning their programme leaflets over and over in their hands, though there was no sign of Pauline Badger. It wasn't simply a middle-aged crowd, as I soon discovered by speaking briefly with a twenty-something man in a faded band T-shirt and black trilby, who explained how awesome the true crime community could be and how excited he'd been for his first Crime Con. He'd arrived with two of his friends from their home in a Glasgow satellite town, though he didn't really have any thoughts on Bible John or anything like that. He was just excited to meet like-minded people, he told me, before bounding off into the talk that was about to begin.

On stage, a handsome thirty-something man in a waist-coat was explaining exactly what his job as a forensic psychiatrist entailed. It wasn't really like the movies, he stressed, though it was certainly eventful in its own way. The talk centred on the 'not guilty by reason of insanity' plea and what it meant in reality, rather than myth. Juicy case studies were offered up to an appreciative audience, before a lengthy plug for his debut book, *In Two Minds: Stories of Murder, Justice and Recovery from a Forensic Psychiatrist*. Dr Sohom Das wanted us to know that he had very little time for psychiatrists who were looking to establish lucrative media careers and that we should treat them with appropriate suspicion. Though that rule didn't count for him of course, he hastened to add with well-oiled comic timing, to a ripple of light applause and laughter. The book was essential reading for anyone with an interest in true crime or mental illness and it didn't end there, we were assured. 'Buy the goddamn book', exhorted the laughing figure on the stage, before pointing us in the direction of his YouTube channel, A Psych For Sore Minds.

David Swindle was due to appear at two discussions, including a panel that promised the full inside story on Peter Tobin, along with Carol Rogers (neé Weston), the forensic scientist who had descended into the depths of St Patrick's Church to attend to Angelika Kluk's body. But first, at 12.15, there was to be another panel highlighting the retired detective's more recent venture, with his team of multilingual experts at David Swindle Crime Solutions and his charity Victims Abroad. I took my place on a row of seats near the back of the room, to watch as a short tribute to Kirsty Maxwell* played on the screen by the stage. The video, haltingly narrated by Maxwell's mother, was short and scrappily produced. She explained a

---

* Twenty-seven-year-old Kirsty Maxwell died in mysterious circumstances on holiday in Benidorm in 2017. The circumstances of her death remain unexplained, while her family have complained of a lack of cooperation from the Spanish authorities.

portion of their family's pain, as photos of a pretty, smiling young woman blurred past. When the screen turned to black, David Swindle said a few words before introducing the Maxwell family. When they'd taken in their polite applause, Kirsty's father stood up to deliver a short speech about his daughter, who had died so senselessly in Spain. All they wanted was the truth, he said, though it still felt very far from their grasp.

As the audience thinned back into the foyer, the call went out that it was time for the buffet lunch. The atmosphere had begun to drift into the vaguely carnivalesque, with most of the natural residual big-crowd awkwardness having evaporated over the course of the morning. David Swindle walked past, though he didn't appear to see my waved greeting. The queue moved slowly, if at all, and the round conference tables began to fill with revellers and paper plates laden with bao buns and pakora, salad and huge fluffy potato wedges. The morning's programme of murder and unfathomable grief didn't appear to have dulled anyone's appetite. I took a seat with the remainder of the solo crowd and started on my food, before making pleasant small talk with a smartly dressed woman in her early fifties who said she was here for one her favourite writers, who was due to appear after lunch. 'And who was that?' I asked. Her only reply was a slightly pitying smile and a pair of involuntarily raised eyebrows, as if she couldn't quite believe her interlocutor's naivety, or ignorance.

Colin Sutton appeared thirty-five minutes later to a chorus of cheers and stamped feet. The ex-Met Detective Chief Inspector and SIO, billed as 'the Real Manhunter' and introduced as 'the man who needed no introduction', took to the stage and waited for the adulation to subside. A cheery, slightly florid, bald man in his late sixties, Sutton had achieved a rarefied celebrity status in the world of true crime fandom after retiring in 2011 from a long and eventful career in the Met. He had opened a private investigative practice, before penning his wildly popular memoirs. First came 2019's *Manhunt*, the story of Sutton's crucial involvement in the Levi Bellfield case. Bellfield was a serial killer and rapist who was served a whole-life tariff in 2008 and another in 2011, after being found guilty of kidnapping and murdering 13-year-old Milly Dowler in 2002. Sutton had followed the first book's success with another edition of *Manhunt*, this time centred on his role in apprehending Delroy Grant, the south-east London serial rapist who became better known as the Night Stalker: not to be confused, of course, with the infamous LA serial killer Richard Ramirez.

The audience sat rapt as Sutton unfurled his well-honed performance, a mixture of deadpan seriousness and fluid storytelling, mixed with just enough safely ribald asides to keep the mood from curdling entirely at the horror on offer. The audience questions were plentiful and enthusiastic. Some wanted to ask about a specific strain of procedural detail or what Sutton thought of the current state of policing in the UK. Others simply wanted to ask what he thought about Martin Clunes, the actor cast as Sutton in the ITV adaptation of his memoirs. Oh, Martin was a very good guy, Sutton explained. He'd liked his performance very much, though he'd had to occasionally tell the actor to lighten up slightly. As the chair signalled that the session was drawing to a close, another burst of hearty applause rang out as Sutton beamed back appreciatively at his audience.

As Sutton retired from the stage, it had seemed like a decent chance to catch my breath. The Podcast Row sat in the room next door, with a spread of individual tables, each one representing a specific long-running show. Crimepedia jostled for foot traffic with Scottish Murders and the UK True Crime Podcast, among others. The room was almost deserted after Sutton's star turn, though I exchanged an indulgent smile with a man briefly manning the Scottish Murders desk, before helping myself to a respectable handful of branded pens and badges.

The next panel dealt with Scotland's Most Evil Killers. It felt odd that so much of the day had passed without even a cursory mention of Bible John, though it seemed as if this was about to change. The screen flashed up with a who's who of the country's most notorious serial murderers and rapists. Dennis Nilsen sat next to Ian Brady, who was placed by Angus Sinclair (Edinburgh's 'World's End' murderer') and Peter Manuel, while Robert Black (convicted of raping and killing four children) and Peter Tobin shared the space at the bottom of the graphic. Colin Sutton had reappeared, along with another ex-detective who looked to be his slightly younger doppelgänger. Dr Sohom Das also returned with a new addition to the panel, a veteran forensic scientist and research professor at Strathclyde University named Jim Fraser. At once, it felt like a slight strain lay under the panel's surface-level bonhomie. Colin Sutton said he didn't know how to answer a question from the chair about 'the most evil' killer on the list, as the choice was rather like being forced to pick your favourite STD. As the laughter died down, the question bounced to Jim Fraser. No, he didn't really agree with the premise and wasn't sure it was a particularly useful lens through which to talk about these terrible crimes. But if he had to pick a particularly harrowing case from his own career, then he supposed Robert Black would have to be up near the worst he'd seen.

The chair said she knew that there was no way of being in Glasgow and not speaking about Bible John, as an appreciative murmur spread across the room. Did the panel have any thoughts about the terrible killer that had stalked the city in the late 1960s? Most hedged their bets or excused themselves from a case they didn't really know all that much about. It was hard with these old cases, Colin Sutton said, as so much had changed in the decades since. Policing culture and practice. Technology had also advanced beyond belief and it was perhaps just not fair to compare now with then.

Jim Fraser had slightly more to say about the old legend. Though he was no expert, he wasn't quite convinced of the existence of a serial killer at all. It had always been a bit flimsy, he explained. Religion had been everywhere in the Glasgow of the late 1960s, and a well-dressed man reaching for a bit of scripture in conversation wouldn't have been so desperately unusual. Three women had been killed, yes, but there was no overwhelming evidence to suggest an uncaught serial killer. His words were not as enthusiastically greeted as those of his panel-mates had been. The conversation moved on. One thing they could all agree on was that any resolution seemed unlikely now, viewed from the autumn of 2022. When question time came, a middle-aged woman took up the microphone and addressed the room. You say it's unlikely, she opened. But perhaps all the inquiry needed was someone with the skills and nous of Colin Sutton. The laughter turned to cheers, as Sutton waved modestly back.

As the session ended, another break was announced for coffee and book signings. Jim Fraser was already deep in conversation with an audience member by the time I made my way back into the near-empty main room. We spoke briefly and exchanged contact details. He reiterated that he wasn't anything approaching a Bible John expert, though he'd be happy to talk sometime. The same young man I'd seen earlier, his trilby still firmly planted on his head, chatted happily with his friends and a couple of slightly older attendees. The charge of the early afternoon had been replaced with a tranquil contentment, as people contemplated their freshly signed books, or ordered drinks from the bar. Though few people had left the third floor, it seemed quieter, or perhaps just less frantic after Colin Sutton's appearance. In the weeks after, I'd read that the crowd had peaked at 500, though it hadn't felt as packed as all that. Perhaps it was just that a cosiness had descended, which almost verged on the conspiratorial.

After almost seven hours at the Hilton, I wasn't sure how many more panels I had left in me, though there was one that I'd circled as unmissable, weeks before. At 5 p.m. sharp, David Swindle arrived on stage with Susie Fraser and Carol Rogers. The talk covered mostly familiar ground. Tobin's crimes and Operation Anagram, Swindle's role in it all and his belief that Tobin had likely killed more victims than he had been charged with, or perhaps ever would be. There was the explanatory section and the myth-busting one. He poured scorn on the suggestion that Tobin had killed forty-eight people, or that he had a link to the supposed Bible John murders. It was simply lazy reporting that had built the first into myth, while the second never really had much basis in fact to begin with.

At the very start of the session, space had been devoted to the lives of Angelika Kluk, Vicky Hamilton and Dinah McNicol. The screen was lit up to show their smiling faces, from the familiar pictures that had become synonymous with their names over the years. The three smiling young women who barely had the chance to become themselves. Susie Fraser asked for a moment of reflection and wondered if the audience knew about the church a few hundred yards from the entrance of the Hilton Hotel. There were nodded heads and a minority of blank looks. It was St Patrick's, the same church where Angelika Kluk's body was found in 2006.

An unignorable hush had descended when Carol Rogers began to speak about her role in securing the desperately needed evidence from the badly battered body that had been discovered under the floorboards. She had only been in the job for a few years when the call came in, though no one needed to tell her what rested on her success or failure. Rogers spoke clearly and without any unnecessary flourishes about the eerie focus and calm that had descended on her. Any trace of the previous jocularity in the audience vanished. When it came time for questions, a figure near the front asked whether she'd been nervous or scared. Rogers said that it hadn't really come into it at the time. There was a job to do, and it had to be done right. Justice, or something like that, had depended on it.

When the talk ended and the applause died out, I said my polite goodbyes and waited for the lift that would take me down to the ground floor and back out into the fresh air. The sky was a dull metallic shade of grey, though the early evening light still stung my eyes after a day of the conference room's artificial rays. St Patrick's squatted to my left, as I walked past the Mitchell Library and up into the West End, where I was due to meet some friends to talk about anything other than serial killers, or murder, or young women brought to the most terrible, pointless endings.

THE LETTER

The weeks after Glasgow Crime Con passed quietly enough, just as the ones before them had. On 12 September, I'd finally packed my suitcase and caught the train back home to London on an overcast and nothingy Monday night. The month in Glasgow had passed easily enough, though without any really sustained distraction or release from Bible John. To the end, I had kept to the same tightly regulated schedule. Up early to pore through the previous day's notes and writing before setting off from my sublet in Mount Florida, around fifteen minutes' walk from the red sandstone tenement that Patricia Docker had once shared with her parents and young son. From the Southside, I'd catch the train into town and make the fifteen-minute journey by foot to the Mitchell Library, to begin the day afresh at 9.30 a.m. The morning would pass with the same stack of books and microfilm, or by my transcribing the latest interview, before I tried to distil the bulky mass of information into something comprehensible during the afternoons. When this routine ran smoothly, I could leave the fifth floor a contented man at 7.30 p.m., before making the reverse trip to Mount Florida.

This was how the days passed. The airlessness made sense, or seemed to make sense to me then. It felt like paying due fidelity to the story and its litany of false starts and dead ends. The white noise and dud theories in the margins that required ever-greater attention to unpick and rethread together into a recognizably orderly narrative. When the library shut on Friday evenings, I'd meet some friends for a drink, before spending the weekend afternoons walking around the city, from what struck me as an increasingly depressed centre, and out east to the Gallowgate and occasionally beyond. The Barrowland would always loom into view as it had done for countless revellers over the decades, the same grand old venue that had reopened after the 1958 fire that had warped and gutted its original iteration. It wasn't difficult to stand outside and imagine the chaos and often frenetic energy of the supposed glory days described in the old histories and chronicles of the city's past. The tail-end of the mythical golden age of immaculately dressed innocence, where a night at the dancing would set you back a few shillings for entry and a bus or taxi home at the end of the night.

Where beaming men and women in their best clothes poured in and out from the inner city and beyond, right back to the freshly built schemes and estates on the city's outer fringes.

This is a myth that often acknowledges its own darker side and its muddier, uglier clichés. The dizzying rate of social change and accompanying fear and isolation that had set in by the late 1960s. The rise in violent crime that seemed to be sweeping across Glasgow like a bout of fever, so adroitly packaged and disseminated by a powerful and brashly self-confident tabloid press. It was right there to read about every day almost without fail, at breakfast or dinner, whether morning or darkest night. The latest teenaged gang member who had it coming, stabbed to death in a brief bout of hellish urban warfare. Or the occasional angelic female innocent found killed in an overgrown and lonely cemetery. The victims grouped into the deserving and undeserving dead alike. Bible John captured the mood and gave shape to it. It gave a name to the anxieties rippling through the city. It made sense, in its own powerfully modern way. There was no doubt that it was inspired work from John Quinn, or whoever else might or might not have been responsible for the coinage of the name. A name so simple and clear. The terrible red-haired figure that stalked the night, quoting scripture and searching for married women to seduce and murder outside their own homes. This spectre was far easier to understand and accept than a city where violence was becoming a threat or a fact of daily life for so many.

It was often said that it could have been anyone, a saying that cuts straight to the heart of the story's power. Whether the work of one man or three, there was never any shortage of plausible killers, or potential suspects. Perhaps the crimes would have been forgotten had there been an ending, the killer finally caught and paraded to the press. Justice served and a real name to finally replace the one bestowed by the tabloids. But there was no ending, and it is vanishingly unlikely that there will be now. No closure or final reckoning with these specific killings from an increasingly distant past. Almost from the moment of his christening, the figure of Bible John had become more than the supposed killer of three women who had each spent their last night dancing at The Barrowland Ballroom. He had become a legend.

* * *

I'd long decided that I wanted to end my reporting in Margate, the small and sometimes self-consciously trendy seaside town on the Kent coast. In October 2020, an interview with a local woman named Abigail Dengate had appeared on the Kent Online website. The 38-year-old mother-of-three had lived at 50 Irvine Drive for eleven years with her children and their grandfather. Of course she'd known the history and what the house represented, but none of that mattered faced with her own far more pressing needs, having lived in wildly overcrowded accommodation. The fact that Peter Tobin had once lived there didn't bother her and nor did what had been discovered buried at the end of the narrow little garden. Her family had moved in in 2009 and were happy in their home, even eleven years later. The murder house epithet just didn't bother her, or her children. They had needed a suitable place to stay, and Thanet Council had been happy to oblige, when it became clear that knocking down the mid-terrace house was too impractical a solution to a fairly unique problem (the previous tenants had almost immediately vacated the property following the discovery of Vicky Hamilton's and Dinah McNicol's remains). I felt that I needed to speak with her, for reasons I barely yet understood. She seemed to encapsulate something about the distinction between the horrors of the past and the often-mundane facts of the present. How life didn't always conform to the expectations you might place on it.

The sun was starting to set when the train left Peckham Rye station on Friday, 7 October 2022. It had been a bright autumn day which held the promise of a cold, crisp night. The Thameslink train to Sevenoaks was still busy with the last of the suburban commuter crowd heading out into the furthest edges of South London and beyond. A couple of visibly exhausted men in paint-splattered work clothes sat at my table, silently sipping at bottles of beer before alighting at Bellingham. To my right, an excitable boy still clad in his school uniform was explaining his week to his smiling mother in exhaustive and rapid-fire detail. At Bromley South, I scooped up my overnight bag and crossed the station to platform 4, where the train to Margate was already loitering. The hour-and-a-half journey passed peacefully enough, as I busied myself with the notes on my laptop, before staring out at the darkened fields which melted past and briefly merged with a succession of small Kent towns, illuminated by soft yellow streetlights and the occasional flickering pub sign.

It had just gone 8.30 when the train finally pulled into an almost deserted Margate station. The streets were quiet save for a few lone walkers, hurrying towards or away from the town centre. Dreamland, the vast modern seaside amusement park, looked tired and off-season empty despite its glaringly vivid neon logo lit up against the darkness. The beach was already entirely shrouded by the night, the sea only visible as a steady shifting mass, slightly inkier black than the sky. At my High Street

Airbnb, I unpacked my laptop and began to read. The quiet was almost total save for a couple of muffled closing-hour arguments that drifted in through the window from the takeaway over the road.

I read from the start. Right through from February 1968, with the discovery of Patricia Docker's body in the suburban lane a few hundred yards from her home. I read again about the failures of the subsequent police inquiry and the fact of her name slowly drifting from the papers. Just another woman killed before gradually fading out of the public eye. The limits of attention set against the perpetual multiplication of horrors, day in, day out, until her name was relegated to the list of all the other unsolved murders that had begun to gather dust on the desks of the city's detectives. 'The nurse' had been news, right up until she wasn't. Right up until the trail behind her had frozen and there was nothing new for the press to write or report on. I thought about her son, the little boy fleetingly referenced in contemporary news reports, who had lived and grown up with his father and stepmother. His mother hadn't died. She was killed, though her murder wasn't destined to remain shrouded in obscurity like the other women who found their likenesses pinned to the unsolved board across 1968.

I looked across the surviving publicly accessible photos of Patricia Docker and reread the brief testimony of her son, talking at various points across the decades in short and unsparing sentences, which were always moving and devoid of any trace of self-pity. I tried and failed again to comprehend even some of what it must have meant, to grow up under the shadow of a murdered mother. It was around eighteen months later when Jemima MacDonald was found in the miserable tenement, yards from the home she had shared with her children. How the same story had played out in the aftermath of her killing, marked by the same public police appeals for witnesses and information. How it had briefly commanded the tabloids, before dropping down the running order and out of the papers entirely. MacDonald was just another woman who had taken her life in her own hands, it was subtly implied from the start. She had been a regular at the notorious Over-25s night at the Barrowland and everyone knew what sort of people those Thursdays catered to. The murder of the 'single mother of three' was sad and shocking, but it didn't remain news any longer than Patricia Docker's had, though the two were eventually causally linked by a few reporters and media-friendly detectives. They had both been at the Barrowland and had both been strangled to death – though that's as far as it went, until Helen Puttock was found by the dog walker in Scotstoun on 1 November 1969, down the street from where she'd lived with her children and often-absent soldier husband.

I thought about what it meant to bring Jemima Mac-Donald into focus yet again, trying to add fresh detail to the flat and threadbare portrait that had emerged over the decades. Was it in honour of her memory, or could another motive be lying somewhere beneath the surface? Of the three families, none had been as explicit in their condemnation of the cottage industry that had developed around Bible John. They had never wanted anything much to do with the speculation or the endless adaptations of their grief. It doesn't really matter what the author's intention might be, or what the work sought to achieve: all they desired was that their mother's and aunt's and sister's murder would stay out of the media and for her memory to finally be allowed to settle into the past. And here I was, yet another writer dredging up half a century of memories and pain. What did it mean, even now, to bring someone's life back into view, when their descendants wanted nothing more or less than privacy?

Surely there is the right to be forgotten, whatever the weight of public fascination or revulsion that surrounded the killing. I thought of the scorn I'd felt at the contemporary news reports and their occasional misogyny, as well as the carelessness of their assumptions. Crime sold, as

Arnot McWhinnie told me straightforwardly over the phone, just as well then as it did today. Maybe the question of motive was simpler then. There were papers to sell and a ready-made audience to engage. The city was your lifeblood and Bible John was a quick guarantee of its attention. To blame the papers for the hysteria would be like blaming the scorpion for its nature. Reporters understood their assignment and precisely what the job entailed. Bible John was like few things that had gone before, though it helped set the template for so much of the crime coverage that was to come in Glasgow and beyond. And the longer that the apparent serial killer stayed uncaught, the more opportunities presented themselves, as each decade threw up its own prime suspect to be pored over and scrutinized, from the beleaguered ex-pat David Henderson in the 1980s, through to the John McInnes fiasco in the mid-1990s.

Legends are supposed to have their heroes, but Bible John never really had one to set against the vividly painted folk devil. The story was always too murky and complex, too fevered and weird to have space for any avenging angels. Joe Beattie was never that figure, however strenuously he'd tried to cast himself in the role. It is not an accident that the former Detective Superintendent has stayed synonymous with the murders. From late 1969 onwards, he had bound himself tightly to the developing saga, far beyond any reasonable justification. There is the temptation towards pity for a figure who was consumed by the legend and who did so much to stoke its formation. One imagines the hangdog, tweed-suited detective down at his Marine Division fiefdom in Partick, poring through the terrible mass of files and photographs until the early hours, drowning slowly under the weight of his burden. One can almost feel the rising dread and anxiety as it must have become apparent, even to his strongest and most committed supporters, and perhaps even to the man himself, that none of the press appeals or desperate curveball tactics was going to take them to the killer. And one wonders if the obsession ever really abated, long after his retirement to a life alternating between comfort and ill health in Bearsden, before his death in 2000, aged 82. The news reports and occasional interviews over the years don't give the impression of a man who could ever let the spectre go, though by the time of McInnes's exhumation in 1996, he had decided that he had never believed in the existence of a serial killer after all.

I thought about Helen Puttock and the family she had left behind. George Puttock, now old and frail, though still occasionally active in the media, responding to the latest stories and updates, still closely guarding his own corner of the narrative. As of 2021, he had told the *Daily Record* that he had never believed in the idea of a serial killer either, though that isn't what is borne out by his previous appearances in the press. Perhaps none of this really mattered. I thought about what Helen Puttock's murder had done to his family. How his eldest son, David, was now in his late fifties and had built a life in Canada, though had still consented to a spring 2022 interview in the *Daily Record* pleading with Police Scotland to do something, anything, to finally solve the story of his mother's murder. His father, he told the paper, deserved that at least. Earlier, 2020 had seen the death of his younger brother Michael who, George Puttock told the press, had never managed to come to terms with the facts of his mother's death. There had been a time, in fact, as a young boy when he had accused his own father of being responsible after a schoolfriend had let slip that his mother had been strangled rather than hit by a bus, as George Puttock had told his children.

I thought about Jeannie Williams, whose sister had been killed, and the life she must have led in the months and years after their Thursday night out at the Barrowland had long passed into myth. How many times must she have repeated the outline of that night to Joe Beattie and his detectives, until she'd given them the story they wanted, as well as to the countless journalists who had appeared at her door in the decades after, right up until her death in 2010. She was transfigured into a character too. The star witness and grieving sister, who had come face to face with the killer himself and lived to describe him into legend.

As the night drew in, I tried to think again on my own role in reanimating the old murders and dragging them back out for another bout of public re-examination. After all the months that had passed, there was no point in lying to myself. Yes, I'd wanted to give more voice to the women who had died and try to improve on the thin attention their lives had received. And I'd tried to paint a picture of the time and place that Bible John had arrived in, and what the enduring fascination with the killings could or couldn't say about our wider fascination with historic crime, or cold cases, or whatever other euphemism that might be wrapped around the fact of three women murdered in Glasgow between February 1968 and November 1969.

Though I had done all of this and much else to try and treat their stories with respect, there was the same shadow that had hung over the undertaking, just as it had at the very beginning of my reporting. The same repelled fascination with the unsolved and probably unsolvable mystery, which made looking away an impossibility. Then there were the predictable, if guilty and involuntary, pleasures of discovering a long-forgotten flourish of detail in an old newspaper, or of tracking down a source who might be able to shed light on a contentious point of fact. The professional pride to be taken in any story, whatever the horror at its core. I thought about what this might say and whether any of what I thought really mattered at all.

I woke up early the next morning after a disturbed sleep, hazy with nightmares and odd sounds I couldn't quite place, which had come from somewhere just outside the bedroom window. Bold yellow sunlight poured through the blinds as I made some tea and skimmed over the literary magazine I'd packed, before heading out for a brief walk across the beach. The rest of the morning passed uneventfully enough, as I continued to read through my Bible John notes, old and new. By early afternoon, the internet in the flat had packed in, so I took myself to the nearby library to continue with my work. The building was almost empty, save for a group of chattering girls, no older than 11 or 12. They spoke about football and schoolwork and laughed loudly at their own increasingly absurd jokes and giddiness. On the other side of the room sat an elderly man carefully thumbing through a greasy copy of the *Financial Times*, page by painstaking page. The mood was light and vaguely cosy in its own way.

After an hour or so, I set aside my notes and opened a new Word document. At first, I didn't know how to start, or even what it was I was trying to write. It was a letter, yes, but not like one I'd ever tried to compose before. The words just wouldn't come and when they did, I'd swiftly delete them and begin again. What precisely should, or could, you say to a stranger whose house you wanted to visit because it had once been dug up as the former residence of one of the UK's most notorious serial killers? I decided to try and write down the truth as clearly as possible. Starting with who I was: a writer that had spent the last few years working on a book regarding Bible John, the infamous and uncaught figure from Glasgow's twentieth-century history.

There has been a theory for a number of years now that Peter Tobin was Bible John, I explained, though neither I nor anyone truly credible still believed in the connection, and maybe doubted that the serial killer called Bible John had ever really existed at all. The next request may seem strange, I wrote. There is myth and horror, and then there is the reality of everyday life. You have a family and needed a place to live, so why should the house's history have impacted on that? I'd added my mobile number and email address, just in case she would be interested in speaking with me at any point, though I totally understood if it sounded too odd or far-fetched for her liking.

It wasn't long before I felt a hand on my shoulder after I'd finished setting down my strange request on paper. It was my friend David, a Margate resident who had agreed to pick me up and drive me to the nondescript council house on Irvine Drive that Peter Tobin had called home. I'd explained the nature of the errand and he'd immediately been only too happy to help, even though he'd have to come straight from his son's seventh birthday party. After returning from the printer, I clocked the look of astonishment and incomprehension spread across David's face. He gestured to his phone screen without a word, which was opened to a short article on the BBC website. The news had just come in. Peter Tobin had died earlier the same morning at Edinburgh Royal Infirmary aged 76, unrepentant to the very end. The article explained that police officers had attended the death at 6.04 a.m., while David Swindle had been quoted stating his enduring belief that Tobin had more undiscovered victims and that he had been a figure without any respect for humanity.

As we drove the fifteen minutes or so to Irvine Drive, my thoughts turned to the practical and professional. The tabloids would be arriving too, though the worst of me knew that we'd already had a significant head start. Soon enough, the bars and restaurants of Cliftonville melted away and the roads became wider, the front gardens that bit smaller or less ostentatiously well kept. It was just about three o'clock and the afternoon sun was at its peak. We parked up on Irvine Drive and walked past a neat row of identikit 1930s council houses, before arriving at the right door where I took the folded letter from my bag. The approach to the house suggested a well-loved and lived-in home, with a couple of chairs and potted plants by the front door, while a family of smiling papier-mâché skeletons hung from the porch canopy. Halloween wasn't too far off. The letter slid through the letterbox and I turned back to face the sunlight before making my way back up the street. David was standing at the bend in the road as I made my way back to him and picked my pace up to a jog.

ACKNOWLEDGEMENTS

This is a story that couldn't be told without the memories of those that lived through the strange, hyper-charged time that witnessed the construction of Bible John, and I'm immensely thankful to everyone who agreed to speak with me over the past few years. I am also greatly indebted to the kindness and expertise of the staff at the Mitchell Library, one of Glasgow's great institutions. No question was ever too small, or news cutting too obscure. I'd also like to thank staff at the *Daily Record* for their help and allowing me to sit in and pore through their in-house archives. Then there are the many others who helped me track down this or that specific document or scrap of video. I am truly grateful to you all and hope I can repay your kindness in the future.

Many thanks to Edwin Morgan and Carcanet Press for permission to reproduce lines from 'Winter (EM)', from *Collected Poems*.

As always, I'd like to thank my friends and family for their support and making life what it is. I spent much of 2022 in Glasgow writing this book. I'd like to thank Harry Weskin, Hayden Traynor, Fran Gordon, Lewis den Hertog, Sonia Hufton, Connell King and Siobhan Ma for making those months in that beautiful city so enjoyable. At home, I'd like to thank Megan Nolan, Tristan Cross, Charles Olafare, Josh Baines, Michael and Paraic Morrissey, Sean Adams and many others who I won't embarrass in public. Thanks also to my agents, Richard Pike and Kat Buckle. Finally, none of it would be possible without my partner, Lolly Adefope. Thanks for everything, always.